ROSE
DISCIPLESHIP SE

GROWING
FRUITS OF THE SPIRIT

R SE
PUBLISHING

Growing: Fruits of the Spirit
Rose Discipleship Series
©2021 Rose Publishing

Published by Rose Publishing
An imprint of Tyndale House Ministries
Carol Stream, Illinois
www.hendricksonrose.com

ISBN 978-164938-017-3

Contributing Editor: Len Woods
Cover design by Sergio Urquiza

Printed in the United States of America
May 2021, 1st printing

Contents

What Is Discipleship?

A disciple is a person who follows Jesus—to *know* Jesus and his teachings, to *grow* more like Jesus, and to *go* for Jesus, serving others and making new disciples. Simply put, the goal of discipleship is to become more like Jesus.

Healthy discipleship is always integrated. What we *know* in our heads should permeate our hearts and help us grow. *Growing* in the faith can't be separated from knowing truth and going forth to serve others and honor God. *Going* is tied together with knowing God's truth and growing to have the right heart attitude.

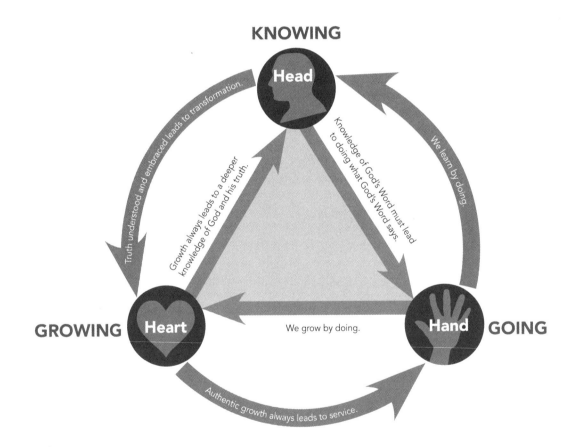

The ten topics in this book focus on *growing* in the fruits of the Spirit and other traits that help us become more like Christ. Other books in this series focus on *knowing* the essential truths about God, the Bible, the gospel, and the church, and *going* forth in service, evangelism, and spiritual practices.

Topic 1: A Disciple Grows

Becoming More Christ-Like

"Being confident of this, that he who
began a good work in you will carry it on to
completion until the day of Christ Jesus."

—Philippians 1:6

You go to your 20-year reunion and, for the most part, it's what you expected: People acting like their lives are better than they really are. Balding classmates trying to one-up each other. Ex-cheerleaders still trying to bask in their high-school glory days. You smile and shake your head. But then, you talk with Eddie, the biggest, most obnoxious jerk from your graduating class. He's had a spiritual conversion. Now, he's humble and genuine. You are stunned at the change.

The next week, while waiting for your daughter to finish her dance class, you're scrolling around on social media on your smart phone. Someone's posted a link to a video about a young woman with a horrific past. As she tells her story, you marvel at how full of joy she is. When she talks convincingly about the Lord giving her the grace to let go of her bitterness and forgive her abuser, you find yourself wiping away tears, genuinely touched by her story.

The promise of the gospel is more than a clean slate with God and the promise of heaven when we die. The gospel gives us radical new life *now*. Being a disciple of Jesus is stepping into that new life, following Jesus, experiencing his transforming presence. "Follow me," Jesus said, "and I will make you become . . . " (Mark 1:17, ESV). In other words, "If you pursue me, expect your life to change."

Accept the gospel. → Follow Jesus. → Experience life change.

We know how important it is to learn about God's Word. However, it's not enough to have only head knowledge of Jesus and the Bible. The goal of the spiritual life isn't accumulating Bible knowledge—the goal is experiencing spiritual transformation!

Bible Study

1. Describe someone you know who has grown spiritually. What did that person act like before and after that growth? How has spiritual growth changed your own life?

_____

_____

_____

_____

_____

2. Consider these passages that speak of God's desire to grow us up in the faith, and make us like his Son:

   > "And as the Spirit of the Lord works within us, we become more and more like him" (2 Corinthians 3:18, TLB).

   > "My dear children, for whom I am again in the pains of childbirth until Christ is formed in you" (The apostle Paul, writing in Galatians 4:19).

   > "But the Holy Spirit produces this kind of fruit in our lives: love, joy, peace, patience, kindness, goodness, faithfulness, gentleness, and self-control" (Galatians 5:22–23, NLT).

   > "Let your roots grow down into him, and let your lives be built on him. Then your faith will grow strong in the truth you were taught, and you will overflow with thankfulness" (Colossians 2:7, NLT).

   What do these verses say about the Lord and his desire for us?

A Definition of *Disciple*

A disciple is a person who follows Jesus—to *know* Jesus and his teaching; to *grow* more like Jesus; and to *go* for Jesus, serving others and making new disciples.

_____

_____

_____

_____

3. The apostle Paul writes, "train yourself to be godly" (1 Timothy 4:7; the NASB renders this phrase "discipline yourself for the purpose of godliness"). What do you think Paul means? Why do you think this is hard?

_____

_____

_____

_____

It's worth noting that the present tense verb Paul uses here (translated "train" or "discipline") is the Greek word from which we get our English term "gymnasium." In other words, Paul is insisting that we give our souls a regular workout! Just as we go to the gym to exercise our bodies, we are to engage in spiritual exercises that will strengthen and firm up our souls.

Such spiritual practices (or holy habits) are often called spiritual disciplines. They are everything from solitude and silence, Bible reading and prayer, to giving and service. *Any regular activity that we intentionally practice in order to open ourselves up to the Lord's transforming presence can be considered a spiritual discipline.*

Just as physical exercise leads to strength and health and fitness, in the same way spiritual exercises, properly understood and utilized, can help us grow to become like Christ.

A wrong view of spiritual disciplines	A right view of spiritual disciplines
Something for monks, nuns, and church leaders	Something for every Christ-follower
Something I am supposed to do for God	A way I can be with God
The goal is doing	The goal is becoming
Performed out of guilt (a "have to")	Practiced out of gladness (a "get to")
An end in themselves	A means to an end—being in God's transforming presence
A sign of spiritual maturity	A means to spiritual maturity

Misconceptions about Growing in God

Transformation Myths	Transformation Truths
Growth is automatic for believers.	Growth has to be pursued.
Maturity is an event or destination.	Maturity is a lifelong process, a journey.
Transformation is entirely up to God.	Transformation ultimately depends on God, but it also requires my participation.
Spiritual progress is mostly about finding and learning the right spiritual information.	Information is one part; "train(ing)" (1 Timothy 4:7), "working out" (Philippians 2:12) and "do(ing)" (James 1:22) are also indispensable. We have to live the truth we know.
Transformation comes from *trying* hard.	Transformation is the result of consistent *training* and constant *trusting* God to empower you.
Following Christ means engaging in a lot of spiritual activities.	The goal of the spiritual life isn't activity; it's intimacy! *Am I learning to love God and love others more and more? Am I taking on the character of Christ?*
God should work in my life exactly the way he's working in another person's life.	Spiritual growth will vary from person to person and from season to season.

4. How is spiritual growth and maturity progressing in your life? Take a few minutes and work through this chart. As you do, consider not just beliefs, but your actions. For example, you may recognize that God's Word is important, but are you reading it?

Tool for Spiritual Growth	Minor factor		Somewhat instrumental			Indispensable to growth			
God's Word	1	2	3	4	5	6	7	8	9	10
The indwelling Spirit of God	1	2	3	4	5	6	7	8	9	10
Relationships/Community	1	2	3	4	5	6	7	8	9	10
Trials and crises	1	2	3	4	5	6	7	8	9	10
Dramatic miracles	1	2	3	4	5	6	7	8	9	10
The passage of time	1	2	3	4	5	6	7	8	9	10
Practicing spiritual disciplines	1	2	3	4	5	6	7	8	9	10
Meeting with a mentor	1	2	3	4	5	6	7	8	9	10
Retreats/Mission trips	1	2	3	4	5	6	7	8	9	10
Prayer	1	2	3	4	5	6	7	8	9	10
Other: _____	1	2	3	4	5	6	7	8	9	10

a. Which of the tools of growth from the chart are you most familiar with? Least familiar with? Did your scoring in any way correspond to how familiar you are with the tool?

_____

_____

_____

_____

_____

_____

_____

b. How does Philippians 1:6, our memory verse for this topic, speak to the whole issue of spiritual growth? What encouragement do you take from it?

_____

_____

_____

_____

_____

_____

_____

c. Referring to the spiritual-growth tools in the chart on page 53, which tool would you like to utilize more in your own spiritual growth? Why? What is one step you can take today toward implementing this tool in your life?

_____

_____

_____

_____

_____

Take-Home Reflections

From Unbelief to Christ-likeness

It's not a cliché. It's a fact: The spiritual life *is* a journey. Coming to Christ and growing to maturity in him is a lifelong process.

At the risk of oversimplifying and over-generalizing, here are some very common, often-observed stages in the spiritual life:

Separated from Christ			New Life in Christ	
unbelief ⟶		✝ faith ⟶	growing pains ⟶	effective service
Skeptic	**Seeker**	**New believer**	**Disciple**	**Disciple-maker**
critical, combative	curious, cautious	confused, childlike	committed, concerned about kingdom matters	Christ-like catalyst for impacting others
What a person in this stage might say:				
"With so much evil in the world, how can you possibly believe in God?"	"I'm so tired of living this way. There must be more to life."	"Where's that verse about God helping those who help themselves?"	"I am praying for an open door to have a spiritual discussion with my neighbor."	"I want to start a discipleship group with two younger women."
What Jesus says to this person:				
"Come!" (*to* me)	"Repent and believe!" (*in* me)	"Follow (*after* me) and become (*like* me)!"		"Go!" (*for* me)
What someone in this stage needs:				
Friendships with authentic believers who model the gospel	A safe place to ask questions about Jesus and his teaching	Relationships with mature believers who demonstrate and explain the basics of the faith	Help in identifying gifts, opportunities to serve with supervision/feedback	A team of co-laborers, lots of encouragement, freedom to fail

Some people might object to making a distinction between "believers" and "disciples." Our intention is to draw attention to the scores of new believers who have not been trained yet to actually follow Jesus. They haven't been shown how to allow Christ to transform their attitudes, values, actions, habits, relationships, finances, etc. So there are true believers who have yet to begin following him and become disciples in the truest sense of the word.

Life Application

An important part of discipleship is learning how to apply God's truths to your life. Below are just a few ways you can start thinking about what you've learned and apply it to your daily life.

1. Memorize our memory verse:

   "Being confident of this, that he who began a good work in you will carry it on to completion until the day of Christ Jesus" (Philippians 1:6).

2. Read Romans 5:3–5. Then spend a few minutes journaling your thoughts about the current problems in your life and how God might be using those to shape you into the image of Christ.

   > "It is the fire of suffering that brings forth the gold of godliness."
   > —Madame Guyon

3. Wrestle with one or two of these questions:

   ▶ What about the idea that "we become like those we spend a lot of time with"? What are the implications of this for a follower of Jesus?

   ▶ The next time trials come, instead of asking the natural, "Why me, God?" question, try asking, "What are you trying to teach me here, Lord?" What kind of difference could this make?

   ▶ In the physical realm, training is easier when you have a trainer and training partners. How do you think this principle might apply to the spiritual realm?

   ▶ Certain things can stunt a person's physical growth. What factors might hinder a person's spiritual growth?

Topic 2: Love

The Hallmark of a Follower of Jesus

"A new command I give you: Love one another.
As I have loved you, so you must love one
another. By this everyone will know that you
are my disciples, if you love one another."
—John 13:34–35

What's the best way to show people you follow Jesus? Wear a cross around your neck? Get a religious tattoo—maybe a Bible verse—in Greek or Hebrew? What about Christian T-shirts or one of those "Jesus fishes" on your vehicle with a catchy bumper sticker just below it?

None of that is wrong. If you feel led to do such things, great. But Jesus indicated his followers should be marked by something much deeper, higher, and more compelling.

Christ called his disciples to love one another—just check out the memory verse for this lesson. Notice what else he said: Loving as *he* loved is what singles us out as his followers. Love is our calling card. Loving others well—even our enemies—is the best case we could *ever* make for the truth of the gospel.

In Mark 1:17 (NASB), Jesus said, "Follow me, and I will *make you become* fishers of men." Bottom-line, he was saying, "Let me change you." In other words, discipleship is more than learning certain truths and participating in various "Christian" activities. Discipleship means becoming like Jesus. It means seeing his character begin to form in our own lives. That character begins and ends with love.

"Love" in the Bible

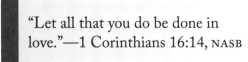

"Let all that you do be done in love."—1 Corinthians 16:14, NASB

The primary Old Testament Hebrew words translated "love" are *ahab* and *chesed*.

Ahab typically means "to desire, delight in, or breathe after" someone or something (as in longing for something). When describing male-female, husband-wife relationships the word may have sexual connotations. However, it is also used to describe:

▷ Parent-child relationships (Genesis 22:2)

▷ In-law relationships (Ruth 4:15)

▷ A servant's love for his master (Exodus 21:5)

▷ The affection between intimate friends (2 Samuel 1:26)

▷ God's love for us (Exodus 20:6; Deuteronomy 7:13)

The other word, *chesed,* is often translated "loving kindness" or "steadfast love" when referring to God's faithful, covenant love for his people—his commitment to show them goodness and favor (Psalm 17:7; 63:3). When used of people, *chesed* is often translated "kindness" or "loyalty" (Genesis 24:49; 2 Samuel 2:5).

In the New Testament, the Greek words *agape* and *phileo* are used to speak of both human and divine love. Some have tried to distinguish sharply between the two, saying that *agape* refers to God's perfect love for us; and *phileo* refers to mere human, brotherly love or friendly affection. But such distinctions oversimplify. In Scripture, there is much overlap. For example, God is said to *phileo* humans (Revelation 3:19). And humans are also encouraged to love (*phileo*) God (1 Corinthians 16:22).

There is much we could say about love, and in this study, we'll be talking about what the Bible says about love.

Bible Study

Biblical Truths About Love

Love originates in God because he is love.

1. Read carefully these verses from 1 John:

> Dear friends, let us continue to love one another, for love comes from God. Anyone who loves is a child of God and knows God. But anyone who does not love does not know God, for God is love.

> God showed how much he loved us by sending his one and only Son into the world so that we might have eternal life through him. This is real love—not that we loved God, but that he loved us and sent his Son as a sacrifice to take away our sins.

> Dear friends, since God loved us that much, we surely ought to love each other. (1 John 4:7–11, NLT)

   a. John tells us here God is the essence of love. Given that this is his *nature*, how does John describe God's *actions*?

   _____

   _____

   _____

   _____

   _____

   b. According to John, what are the expected actions of a child of God?

   _____

   _____

   _____

   _____

   _____

The spiritual life can be boiled down to one word: love.

2. Check out this key passage from Mark's gospel:

> One of the teachers of the law came and heard them debating. Noticing that Jesus had given them a good answer, he asked him, "Of all the commandments, which is the most important?"
>
> "The most important one," answered Jesus, "is this: 'Hear, O Israel: The Lord our God, the Lord is one. Love the Lord your God with all your heart and with all your soul and with all your mind and with all your strength.' The second is this: 'Love your neighbor as yourself.' There is no commandment greater than these." (Mark 12:28–31)

It's worth noting that in the time of Christ, the leaders of Jewish religious culture had dissected the Mosaic Law into 613 individual commandments[1]—365 "don'ts" (one for each day of the year!) and 248 "do's." They argued incessantly over which ones were the most important. And they put in time and effort to make sure they were good Jews: Obeying requirements for food, worship, idols, clothing, work, money, marriage, farming, sex, hairstyles, legal, lending, health, parent-child and employer-employee/slave relationships, mourning, proper sacrifices, priest's duties, and more.

a. Do the people of today's church still argue about rules that should be followed? What rules have you heard others say are important?

_____

_____

_____

b. Jesus reduced 613 rules to one principle, with two parts: *Love God* and *love people*. When life gets complex, and we want to know what rule to follow, Jesus tells us to rely on this guiding principle. Why do we so often find this simplified, straightforward command so difficult to live out?

_____

_____

_____

_____

1 "613 Commandments," *Wikipedia*: https://en.wikipedia.org/wiki/613_commandments (accessed August 8, 2016)

Loving God and loving people are a package deal.

3. Let's look again at 1 John 4:

> If someone says, "I love God," but hates a fellow believer, that person is a liar; for if we don't love people we can see, how can we love God, whom we cannot see? And he has given us this command: Those who love God must also love their fellow believers." (1 John 4:20–21, NLT)

a. These are sobering words! What would you say if someone responded to this verse and said, "Yeah, but my boss—if you knew him, you'd know why I despise him!"?

_____

_____

_____

_____

Even the Ten Commandments illustrate this basic "Love God, Love People" principle. The first four commandments are about loving God, and the final six commandments have to do with relating in love to others. We've seen Jesus highlight this connection in talking about the Great Commandment; John echoes it in his epistle. God doesn't want us to miss this: *We can't separate loving him from loving others!*

> "Do not waste time bothering whether you 'love' your neighbor; act as if you did."—C. S. Lewis

Love is more an action than an emotion.

4. "Dear children, let us not love with words or speech but with actions and in truth" (1 John 3:18). Why is it dangerous to speak of love as a feeling—as something that we fall into or fall out of? Why aren't warm feelings enough?

_____

_____

_____

_____

God's love is sacrificial and unconditional.

5. Read John 3:16.

   a. What was the result of God's great love for the world? Is there such a thing as a love that doesn't cost anything? Why or why not?

_____

_____

_____

_____

   b. Read Romans 8:31–39. List all the things that the apostle Paul says can separate a child of God from God's love. What actions disqualify us from receiving his affection?

_____

_____

_____

   c. What does this tell us about the way we are to love others?

_____

_____

_____

God's love extends even to "enemies."

6. Consider these words of Jesus:

"You have heard that it was said, 'Love your neighbor and hate your enemy.' But I tell you, love your enemies and pray for those who persecute you, that you may be children of your Father in heaven. He causes his sun to rise on the evil and the good, and sends rain on the righteous and the unrighteous. If you love those who love you, what reward

"What does love look like? It has the hands to help others. It has the feet to hasten to the poor and needy. It has eyes to see misery and want. It has the ears to hear the sighs and sorrows of men. That is what love looks like."—Augustine

will you get? Are not even the tax collectors doing that? And if you greet only your own people, what are you doing more than others? Do not even pagans do that? Be perfect, therefore, as your heavenly Father is perfect."
(Matthew 5:43–48)

a. Practically speaking, what does it look like to love an enemy? In day-to-day life? On social media? When talking with friends and the enemy isn't around?

_____

_____

_____

_____

b. Read Jesus' famous Parable of the Good Samaritan in Luke 10:25–37. As you do, remember that the Jews and Samaritans in Jesus' day couldn't stand each other—for historical, racial, and cultural reasons. Where in your own experience have you seen this kind of "risky, unexpected" love?

_____

_____

_____

_____

God's love is jaw-droppingly beautiful!

7. Take a few minutes to slowly read 1 Corinthians 13—often called the "Love Chapter" of the Bible.

> "Love slays what we have been that we may be what we were not."
> —Augustine

a. Why would Paul suggest that spiritual abilities, theological knowledge, or religious actions can actually get in the way of genuine love?

_____

_____

_____

_____

b. Now, read 1 Corinthians 13 a second time, inserting your own name every time you see the word "love." How would your life and relationships be different if you loved like that?

_____

_____

_____

_____

_____

c. What's the most amazing display of love you've ever seen by another person?

_____

_____

_____

_____

_____

Love makes room for those who are different.

Read Romans 14. In this chapter, Paul talks about a common problem of the church. Many followers of Jesus have different convictions about some behaviors not expressly forbidden by God. For first-century believers in Rome, it was the issue of eating meat that had been part of pagan rituals. For modern believers it might be an issue like drinking a beer or a glass of wine.

8. How does love make a difference when Christians have different scruples or standards on issues like these?

_____

_____

_____

_____

_____

Our love can become displaced.

9. Ponder this verse: "Do not love the world nor the things in the world. If anyone loves the world, the love of the Father is not in him" (1 John 2:15, NASB). What does it mean to "love the world"? Why is this a problem? How can a person tell if he or she is in love with "the world"?

_____

_____

_____

_____

We can't love rightly apart from God's enabling Spirit.

In Galatians 5:19–21, Paul talks in depressing detail about all the selfish and wrong ways we act when left to ourselves. Then he writes the phrase, "But the fruit of the Spirit is love" (Galatians 5:22). Here he offers a supernatural possibility—letting God's Spirit reign and rule in us, bringing forth a harvest of love.

What's distinctive about a follower of Jesus? The same virtue that marked our Savior—love. In the strength and security, the wonder and power of Christ's sacrificial, unconditional love for us, we are free to love others. Because we are loved eternally, and perfectly by the Perfect One, we have nothing to fear. We can move toward others to give and serve and bless—just as he did.

We love because he first loved us.

Take-Home Reflections

To Love or Not to Love

Look at this chart to see in what direction a follower of Jesus can direct his or her love.

Things the Bible calls us to love:	Things the Bible warns us NOT to love:
Our neighbor Leviticus 19:18	**Violence** Psalms 11:5
The strangers and foreigners who reside in our midst Leviticus 19:34; Deuteronomy 10:19	**Cursing others** Psalms 109:17
The Lord our God Deuteronomy 6:5; 10:12	**Being simple-minded** Proverbs 1:22
God's salvation Psalms 18:1–2	**Transgression** Proverbs 17:19
Justice Psalms 99:4	**Sleep** Proverbs 20:13
God's law and commandments Psalms 119:47, 97, 113, 127, 140, 167	**Pleasure** Proverbs 21:17
The name of God Psalms 119:132	**Wine** Proverbs 21:17
Wisdom Proverbs 4:5–6	**Money** Ecclesiastes 5:10; 1 Timothy 3:3; 6:10; Hebrews 13:5
Discipline Proverbs 12:1	**Evil** Amos 5:15
Those who reprove or correct us Proverbs 15:12	**Perjury** Zechariah 8:17
Good Amos 5:15	**The approval of others more than the approval of God** John 12:43
Kindness/Mercy Micah 6:8	**This present world** 2 Timothy 4:10; 1 John 2:15
Our enemies Matthew 5:44	
Fellow disciples John 13:34	
All God's people Ephesians 1:15	
(To husbands) **Your wife** Ephesians 5:25; Colossians 3:19	
The Lord Jesus Christ Ephesians 6:24	
Our brothers and sisters in Christ 1 Thessalonians 4:9; Hebrews 13:1; 1 Peter 1:22	
The imminent appearing or second coming of Christ 2 Timothy 4:8	
(To young wives and mothers) **Your husband and children** Titus 2:4	

Life Application

An important part of discipleship is learning how to apply God's truths to your life. Below are just a few ways you can start thinking about what you've learned and apply it to your daily life.

1. Memorize our verse, John 13:34–35.

2. Review this lesson. On a separate sheet of paper, journal your response to this truth: *We will never know how to love until we first know that we are loved.*

3. Practice loving others. We will only become loving people by doing loving acts. Like any skill, getting good at love requires practice and repetition! Pick a couple of the loving acts listed in "Show Your Love" on the next page, or invent your own and try them out this week.

4. Wrestle with one or two of the following:

   ▶ Do you have to *like* somebody in order to *love* them in the way that Christ commands? Why or why not?

   ▶ Is there someone you've treated with cruelty, hatred or violence? If love is a hallmark of Christians, how can you react the next time you're in a similar situation? How can you make things right with the person you've wronged?

   ▶ Do you have an "enemy"? A bully at school, disrespectful boss, mean neighbor, manipulative person, critic on social media, political candidate, or arrogant relative? How can you pray for them and for yourself?

Show Your Love

▷ Secretly serve a roommate, classmate, teacher, coworker, or friend. Identify a need and meet it, without revealing what you have done or taking credit.

▷ Give a loved one a hug for no reason.

▷ Do a dreaded chore for a family member—one that he or she really struggles to complete.

▷ Clear the table—without anyone prompting you.

▷ Wash the dishes or put them in the dishwasher without being asked.

▷ Change that diaper the moment you realize it's dirty and/or wet. Don't wait for someone else to "catch a whiff"!

▷ Offer to run errands for a friend who is frazzled.

▷ Do something sweet for your wife or mother—choose a day other than Mother's Day!

▷ Practice a not-so random act of kindness for a neighbor.

▷ Sneak into someone else's room one morning and make the bed.

▷ Give someone your undivided attention. Ask them questions and really listen for one hour.

▷ Notice a friend's needs. Then meet them before being asked.

▷ Take twenty minutes to sit down and write a letter of encouragement to someone who has marked your life.

▷ Say a prayer for someone you don't get along with or just don't like. Ask God to help you love this person the way that he does.

▷ Identify something that needs to be done that nobody else seems to notice. Go through the proper channels and do it!

▷ Donate your expertise to someone who really needs it.

▷ Take your kids with you to help a friend or family member.

▷ Tithe your waking, non-working, and non-school moments for one week. If that comes to five hours, then that's 300 minutes a week. Agree to spend thirty minutes daily serving someone different for the next seven days.

▷ Gather your small group or discipleship group and secretly go help someone in need.

▷ Pile your family in the car and drive around until you see an elderly person doing yard work. Tell him or her you have two free hours and ask, "How can you use us?"

▷ Offer to babysit for three hours for a harried homemaker.

▷ Clean your dad's vehicle.

▷ Double your portions as you prepare supper and invite a neighborhood family to join you. Or take a meal to an elderly neighbor.

▷ Tutor a kid who's having trouble in school.

Topic 3: Joy & Peace

Life as God Meant for It to Be

"May the God of hope fill you with all joy
and peace as you trust in him, so that you
may overflow with hope by the power of
the Holy Spirit."
—Romans 15:13

When we think about the *qualities* that mark a follower of Jesus, two rare and beautiful virtues that come to mind are *joy* and *peace*.

▷ Bob is a guy who goes to church regularly. He would quickly tell you about his faith in Christ. But if you watched him for very long, you'd soon see he doesn't have a ton of joy in his life. Most days he's tense and fretful—not free and full of peace. There's a heaviness about him that, frankly, is painful to be around.

▷ Tricia on the other hand has a serene and lighthearted quality about her. She doesn't just smile, she's radiant. You know that old hymn "It Is Well with My Soul"? Tricia could be a walking advertisement for that idea. Just being with her is a delight and a comfort.

"Joy is the mark of a true Christian."
—William Wilberforce

Bible Study

Joy: What Is Joy?

The Old Testament Hebrew word *simha* and the New Testament Greek word *chara* convey a deep internal gladness that both comes from and culminates in external expression. In other words, joy is both a condition or quality and an action. We practice it (rejoicing) in order to possess it (joyfulness). True joy inevitably leads to heartfelt rejoicing, and vice versa. Expressions of joy can be individual or corporate, private or public, reserved or exuberant, quiet or noisy. As such, feasting, singing, shouting, dancing, bowing, praying, and laughing are all valid expressions of joy.

Where Does Joy Come From?

1. Take a moment and read Nehemiah 8:10; John 15:11 and 1 Thessalonians 1:6. What strikes you about these verses?

_____

_____

_____

_____

Phrases like "the joy of the Lord" (Nehemiah 8:10), verses where Christ refers to his joy (Luke 10:21; John 15:11; 17:13), and references to the joy of the Holy Spirit (1 Thessalonians 1:6) remind us that *our Triune God is joyful*. When we list his attributes, we are quick to mention how he is holy, just, gracious, omnipotent, loving, sovereign, etc. Not many of us think often about the truth that "God is *joyful!*" But in addition to the verses above, consider Zephaniah 3:17, "The LORD your God is in your midst, A victorious warrior. He will exult over you with joy, He will be quiet in His love, He will rejoice over you with shouts of joy (NASB)."

> "Joy is the serious business of heaven."—C. S. Lewis

Ultimately, just as the Lord is the source of all true love (see "Topic 13: The Hallmark of a Follower of Jesus"), so he is the source of all authentic joy. And because he lives within us by his Spirit, infinite joy is readily available to us even in the midst of hard times. "You have made known to me the path of life; you will fill me with joy in your presence, with eternal pleasures at your right hand." (Psalm 16:11).

How Do We Cultivate Joy?

The fact that we are told, "Always be joyful" lets us know that joy is not exclusively a feeling (1 Thessalonians 5:16, NLT). Rather than being an emotion that comes and goes, joy is a quality that we can cultivate. It is something we can kindle, fan into flame—or, to switch metaphors, harvest: "But the fruit of the Spirit is . . . joy" (Galatians 5:22, NASB).

In the Bible, gladness is always tied to God (see Psalm 32:11; 64:10; 104:34; 126:3; Joel 2:23). At least forty verses connect the *act of rejoicing* with *the state of gladness*. In other words, joy comes from looking beyond temporary circumstances to the unchanging person and promises of God.

In the Bible, we see joy when people:

- Receive an invitation from Jesus (Luke 19:6)
- Hear the news of God's salvation in Christ (Luke 2:10–11)
- Discover the kingdom of heaven (Matthew 13:44)
- Encounter the truth of the empty tomb—Christ's resurrection (Matthew 28:8)
- Hear the teaching of Jesus (John 15:11)
- Experience answers to prayer (John 16:24)
- Spend time with the people of God (Acts 2:46)
- Understand and believe the gospel of Jesus (Acts 8:39)
- Get to be part of spreading the truth of God (Acts 13:38–42)
- Write about and remember their experience with Jesus (1 John 1:4).

Happiness or Joy? What's the Difference?

The Bible doesn't draw a sharp distinction between happiness and joy. In fact, it seems at times to use the words synonymously. But what our culture calls happiness and what the Bible describes as happiness are indeed two different things. Read Psalm 13 (it's short) and then study this chart:

Worldly Happiness	Heavenly Joy
More of an emotion	More of a virtue or character quality
A fickle feeling of giddiness	A settled stance of gladness
Determined by human circumstances	Determined by Godly realities
Gathered from worldly events	Given ultimately by God
Destroyed by difficulties	Shaken but not destroyed by difficulties
Found on the surface of life	Stems from the depths of the heart
Comes and goes	Resides within the hearts of disciples
Something people hope to find	Something people can cultivate

2. How does Psalm 13 illustrate the real possibility of joy despite tough circumstances?

_____

_____

_____

_____

_____

3. What would you say about joy to a friend who battles with ongoing depression?

_____

_____

_____

_____

It's worth noting that a number of the psalms are—well, not the sort of upbeat, peppy "songs" you'd hear in many church services. These raw and honest expressions speak about painful realities and disturbing situations. They *don't* deny the truth that life is often hard; they *do* represent an attempt to remember that in the hard times God is always good and in control.

> "Joy is a continuous, 'defiant Nevertheless.'"—Karl Barth

By holding this tension, the psalms show that joy isn't the result of fickle feelings, but from the choice to put hope in eternal certainties. The psalms teach us that while we don't rejoice *because of* tragedy, we can still be glad *in the midst of it*. How? By trusting that we are held by a God who is with us, who one day will dry every tear.

Rejoicing (the action) is an expression of this faith; it's an exercise in hopeful surrender to God and a refusal to treat temporal circumstances as the final word.

Because of all this, we can experience a kind of quiet confidence—even when life is unpleasant. We don't have to go through life despairing, full of gloom and doom. It seems impossible, but we can grieve current hurts even as we rejoice in future hopes.

As we better understand God's purposes and more willingly embrace them, we can learn and practice gratitude instead of grumbling (James 1:2). Instead of ranting at the world, we can rest and rejoice in God's sovereign care.

31 Simple Ideas for Cultivating Gladness

This weekend declare that it is "Celebration Saturday." Then . . .

1. Loudly say "Amen!" in church.

2. Reflect on God's character—who he is.

3. Review God's works—what he's done.

4. Remember God's promises—what he pledges he will do.[2]

5. Celebrate "little" things: "Madison hit a home run!" "Josh made his bed."

6. Celebrate "big" things—birthdays, anniversaries, promotions, etc.

7. This week, buy or bake a dessert for *no* reason or for *any* and *every* reason.

8. Throw confetti.

9. Celebrate in small groups.

10. Have a festival: a barbecue, potluck, neighborhood block party, etc.

11. Cheer more often for the little blessings of life.

12. Notice God's creation. Shake your head in wonder. Stop and marvel.

13. Don't be so serious! Lighten up! Be silly!

14. Joke around more. Let your playful side come out.

15. Smile more often.

16. Find and hang out with joyful people.

17. Look back at family pictures and old videos.

18. Become a better laugher. Chuckle. Giggle. Laugh. *Belly* laugh. Guffaw. Cackle. Hoot. Snort. Roll on the floor.

19. Give high fives and fist bumps.

20. Cry tears of joy at God's goodness.

21. Lead others in giving three cheers.

22. Throw spontaneous dance parties.

23. Play the thankful game.

24. Pray for a cheerful attitude.

25. Ask God's Spirit to grow the virtue of "joy" in your life (Galatians 5:22)—then work with him to harvest it.

26. With an accountability partner, remove the habit of grumbling from your life (see Philippians 2:14).

27. Embark on a mission to stop being pessimistic and focus on the positive.

28. Buy or borrow some praise CDs.

29. Sing. Sing loudly. Sing like you mean it.

30. Think about the words you're singing when singing worship songs.

31. If you're a hugger, hug someone.

2 "God's Bible Promises," *Bibleinfo.com*: http://www.bibleinfo. com/en/topics/bible-promises (accessed August 8, 2016).

4. Which of these things do you do? Not do? Which ones will you choose to do this week?

Peace: What Is Peace?

5. Take a moment to ponder this verse:

"You will keep in perfect peace all who trust in you, all whose thoughts are fixed on you!" (Isaiah 26:3, NLT)

a. What's the promise here?

The most common term for peace in the Old Testament is the well-known Hebrew word *shalom*. It is used more than 350 times, and it is an unbelievably rich word, with a wide range of connotations.

Depending on the context *shalom* can refer to **wholeness** and **intactness, health** and **well-being,** or **security** and **prosperity.** Shalom speaks of **blessing** and **joy, vitality** and **fruitfulness, community** and **harmony**. And if all that weren't enough, it's **neighborliness,** deep **satisfaction** and **rest**.

Look at those words in the definition of *shalom*. Ponder them. *Shalom*, God's peace, means so much more than "things are okay."

Real peace, God's peace, isn't just the *absence* of visible tension and conflict, it is the *presence* of deep wholeness and joy. Shalom is "life to the full" (John 10:10). Shalom is what we get when we experience life rooted in a right relationship with a good and holy, all-powerful, all-wise God.

b. Where is your life marked by God's *shalom*? Where is it not?

_____

_____

_____

The reason God's offer of peace is so beautiful is because we live in world that is shattered by sin, not permeated with *shalom*. The good news, the gospel, tells us that Jesus, "the Prince of Peace," came to bring *shalom*! Let's look briefly at three kinds of peace we can enjoy as followers of Jesus:

Eternal Peace

6. Read Luke 2:14. What was the angelic announcement to the shepherds about the birth of Christ?

_____

_____

Many Christmas cards render this verse "peace on earth, good will toward men," but the most literal translation of the angelic announcement is "peace to men on whom his favor (grace) rests." In other words, peace with God. A right relationship with God. Acceptance. Forgiveness. Salvation, by grace alone, through faith in Christ alone (Ephesians 2:8–9).

Someone has said that in the birth of Christ, God offered the world a peace treaty. And in his death at the cross, Christ signed that treaty in his own blood.

Do you feel a need for such peace? The assurance that you are right with God? If so, review "Topic 4: Assurance of Salvation."

Interpersonal Peace

7. Consider the meaning of this verse: "If it is possible, as far as it depends on you, live at peace with everyone" (Romans 12:18).

a. How would you explain this verse to a child?

_____

_____

_____

b. When is it not possible to have peace with others?

_____

_____

_____

Because God has taken the initiative to make peace with us, we can follow in the footsteps of Jesus—and take the initiative to move toward our "enemies" and seek peace.

8. How are things going in your life with having peace with others? Look at the scale below and plot your key relationships right now—with a spouse (if married), parents, children, coworkers, neighbors, friends, fellow church members, etc.

A Relational Peace Scale

war		enmity		conflict		mistrust		tension		neutrality		civility		cordiality		harmony		trust		love
-10	-9	-8	-7	-6	-5	-4	-3	-2	-1	0	1	2	3	4	5	6	7	8	9	10

a. Which of your personal relationships need work? And what specifically does that "work" call for on your part?

_____

_____

_____

_____

Internal Peace

9. Read Philippians 4:6–7. What do these verses tell us about how to experience internal peace; the peace *of* God within our own hearts and souls?

_____

_____

_____

Because God is the source of true joy and real peace, followers of Jesus can experience these realities, and see them grow in our lives. We can be different when we work with the One who works in us!

Take-Home Reflections

Trouble-ometer Indicate how much difficulty you are experiencing right now in the following categories—the lower the number, the greater the trouble.	Things are hopeless!	Continual crisis	Paralyzed by fear	Constant high stress	Significant problems	Moderate unease	Bumps in the road	Minor heartburn	No real complaints	Total peace and joy!
My relationship with my parents	1	2	3	4	5	6	7	8	9	10
My marriage	1	2	3	4	5	6	7	8	9	10
The welfare of my children	1	2	3	4	5	6	7	8	9	10
My job/career situation	1	2	3	4	5	6	7	8	9	10
My financial condition	1	2	3	4	5	6	7	8	9	10
My physical health	1	2	3	4	5	6	7	8	9	10
My closest friends	1	2	3	4	5	6	7	8	9	10
My neighbors	1	2	3	4	5	6	7	8	9	10
My teachers/administrators	1	2	3	4	5	6	7	8	9	10
My coworkers	1	2	3	4	5	6	7	8	9	10
My academic situation	1	2	3	4	5	6	7	8	9	10
My overall emotional state	1	2	3	4	5	6	7	8	9	10
My connection with God	1	2	3	4	5	6	7	8	9	10
My overall feeling about my life (where I'm headed, etc.)	1	2	3	4	5	6	7	8	9	10

Life Application

An important part of discipleship is learning how to apply God's truths to your life. Below are just a few ways you can start thinking about what you've learned and apply it to your daily life.

1. Memorize our verse, Romans 15:13.

   "May the God of hope fill you with all joy and peace as you trust in him, so that you may overflow with hope by the power of the Holy Spirit."

2. Using a concordance, survey all the Bible verses that contain the words *joy* and *peace*. What additional insights does this quick study give you into these virtues?

3. Do you have conflict with another person that you can set aside and "agree to disagree" in order to have peace?

4. Wrestle with one or both of the following:

   ▶ Look at the chart on page 141. What can you do to experience God's peace and joy despite your current difficulties?

   ▶ Read and ponder 1 Thessalonians 2:19–20; 3:9 and Psalm 16:3. How do other believers contribute to our joy? How have you seen this in your life?

Topic 4: Patience, Kindness, & Goodness

Enjoying Radical Relationships

"The fruit of the Spirit is love, joy, peace,
forbearance, kindness, goodness,
faithfulness, gentleness and self-control.
Against such things there is no law."

—Galatians 5:22–23

It was former heavyweight champion Mike Tyson who famously said, "Everybody has a plan until they get punched in the face." That wry observation isn't just true of boxing. We could also apply it to our relationships.

> "This is the whole of Christianity. There is nothing else. . . . It is easy to think that the Church has a lot of different objects—education, building, missions, holding services. . . . The Church exists for nothing else but to draw men into Christ, to make them little Christs. If [we] are not doing that, all the cathedrals, clergy, missions, sermons, even the Bible itself, are simply a waste of time. God became man for no other purpose."—C. S. Lewis, *Mere Christianity*

How *easy* it is for disciples of Christ to study and discuss great biblical concepts like love. How *hard* it is to be loving when we step into the arena of marriage or work! According to Galatians 5:22–23, our lives— and our interactions with others—can and should be marked by supernatural patience, kindness, and goodness. How does this happen? What's involved in receiving such graces from God, cultivating them, and then sharing them with others around us?

We're examining the qualities that mark a follower of Jesus.

It's worth repeating: discipleship isn't just studying the Bible and engaging in religious activities. Rather, it involves a slow, steady transformation into Christ-likeness. In other words, it isn't simply knowing and doing new things; it's becoming the new people God created us to be.

Before we look at how the Bible describes patience, kindness, and goodness, take a shot at defining them yourself.

Patience:

_____

Kindness:

_____

Goodness:

_____

In our study today, we'll examine how the Bible uses these terms.

Bible Study

Patience

The most common Old Testament Hebrew word translated "patience" comes from a verb that means "to be long." The idea is that one with this virtue takes a long time to get riled up. In other words, he or she is "slow to anger."

In the New Testament two primary Greek words convey the idea of patience. The first, _hypomené_, means to "remain under"—to remain steady during tests and trials. It is often translated "endure" or "persevere" without grumbling or complaining.

The other word, _makrothumia_, refers to patience as the ability to bear, tolerate, or put up with others without becoming provoked. The word suggests restraint, being slow to speak and slow to become angry (James 1:19).

1. Check out Nehemiah 9:17. This verse discusses divine patience:

   "They [the ancient people of Israel] refused to listen, and did not remember Your wondrous deeds which You had performed among them; so they became stubborn and appointed a leader to return to their slavery in Egypt. But You are a God of forgiveness, gracious and compassionate, slow to anger and abounding in lovingkindness; and You did not forsake them." (Nehemiah 9:17, NASB)

   What stands out to you most about this description of God?

   _____

   _____

   _____

The Bible tells us that "God is love" (1 John 4:8) and that "Love is patient" (1 Corinthians 13:4). Logically, it follows then that *God is patient.*

The apostle Paul wrote: "But God had mercy on me so that Christ Jesus could use me as a prime example of his great patience with even the worst sinners. Then others will realize that they, too, can believe in him and receive eternal life" (1 Timothy 1:16, NLT).

It wasn't just Paul. God is infinitely patient with all of us! He does not treat us as our sins deserve (Psalm 103:10). He is restrained, slow to become angry. He waits and delays judgment because he is merciful (2 Peter 3:9).

Can you believe such good news? Because God is essentially patient, he is always patient *with us.* Not only this, but because the perfectly patient One now *indwells us by his Spirit,* we have what it takes to be patient with others. Look at what God's Spirit inspired the apostle Paul to command:

> "Therefore, as God's chosen people, holy and dearly loved, clothe yourselves with compassion, kindness, humility, gentleness and patience. Bear with each other and forgive one another if any of you has a grievance against someone. Forgive as the Lord forgave you." (Colossians 3:12–13)

2. How would you rate yourself 1–5 in the area of patience?

   ▷ 1 = I can't help expressing disgust when things don't go right. I get angry, yell at people and threaten their job.

   ▷ 2 = I don't express disgust openly but I think incompetent people are worthless.

   ▷ 3 = I accept that there are delays, misunderstandings, malfunctions, and situations in life that go wrong. I can tolerate some problems.

   ▷ 4 = I realize there may be reasons for problems that aren't evident and accept that most people are doing the best they can.

   ▷ 5 = I do my best to keep a positive attitude and keep going. I don't lose my temper. I know God has a purpose for delays, frustrations, and problems.

   Why would you rate yourself that way?

   _____

   _____

   _____

Patience is a wonderful virtue. We admire it when we see it in others. We'd all agree it's a behavior we'd like to exhibit more often. So we study it, and ask God to help us have it. And do our best to have patience the next time life punches us in the face!

Kindness

In the New Testament, a number of Greek words express the idea of kindness.

▶ One New Testament Greek word translated "kindness" is the word *philanthropia* from which we get our English word philanthropy. It means "love for mankind" and suggests providing generously to others. This is the word found in Acts 28:2.

▶ Another word is the word *philadelphia*, which refers to "brotherly affection that results in acts of kindness" (Romans 12:10; 2 Peter 1:7).

▶ A third is the Greek word translated simply "kindness" in Galatians 5:22, *chrestotes* (see also Ephesians 2:7), which can also be translated "good" (as in Romans 3:12).

▶ In "Topic 2: Love," we saw one of the words translated "love" is also translated "kindness." This word, *chesed*, is often translated "loving kindness" or "steadfast love" when referring to God's faithful, covenant love for his people (Psalm 17:7; 63:3). When used of people, *chesed* is often translated "kindness" or "loyalty" (Genesis 24:49; 2 Samuel 2:5).

Put all this together and the idea behind the concept of biblical kindness is a kind of benevolent friendliness and sympathy that gets richly expressed in words and deeds. In other words, kindness isn't just a warm feeling, it is action on behalf of another.

Look at this verse that speaks of an unusually kind woman: "Now in Joppa there was a disciple named Tabitha (which translated in Greek is called Dorcas); this woman was abounding with deeds of kindness and charity which she continually did" (Acts 9:36, NASB).

3. Who in your life would you say "abounds in kindness"?

_____

_____

_____

As with patience, kindness finds its ultimate expression in God's actions toward us:

▶ "Or do you show contempt for the riches of his kindness, forbearance and patience, not realizing that God's kindness is intended to lead you to repentance?" (Romans 2:4).

▶ "But God is so rich in mercy, and he loved us so much, that even though we were dead because of our sins, he gave us life when he raised Christ from the dead. (It is only by God's grace that you have been saved!) For he raised us from the dead along with Christ and seated us with him in the heavenly realms because we are united with Christ Jesus. So God can point to us in all future ages as examples of the incredible wealth of his grace and kindness toward us, as shown in all he has done for us who are united with Christ Jesus" (Ephesians 2:4–7, NLT).

4. List some of the specific ways God has shown kindness to you.

_____

_____

_____

_____

_____

Given God's immense kindness to us (Colossians 1–2), Paul discusses how followers of Jesus ought to respond (Colossians 3–4). In Colossians 3:12–13, he writes:

"Therefore, as God's chosen people, holy and dearly loved, clothe yourselves with compassion, kindness, humility, gentleness and patience. Bear with each other and forgive one another if any of you has a grievance against someone. Forgive as the Lord forgave you."

> "Be kind. Everyone you meet is fighting a hard battle."—Author unknown (variously attributed to Plato, Philo of Alexandria, Ian Maclaren, John Watson)

5. What does to "clothe yourself with . . . kindness" mean to you?

_____

_____

_____

_____

Goodness

Consider the following passages that discuss *goodness*:

▶ "The LORD is good to everyone. He showers compassion on all his creation" (Psalm 145:9, NLT).

▶ "And concerning you, my brethren, I myself also am convinced that you yourselves are full of goodness, filled with all knowledge and able also to admonish one another" (Romans 15:14, NASB).

> "So then, while we have opportunity, let us do good to all people, and especially to those who are of the household of the faith" (Galatians 6:10, NASB).

> "So we keep on praying for you, asking our God to enable you to live a life worthy of his call. May he give you the power to accomplish all the good things your faith prompts you to do" (2 Thessalonians 1:11, NLT).

> "In the same way, let your light shine before others, that they may see your good deeds and glorify your Father in heaven" (Matthew 5:16).

6. What do these verses say about the Lord's character, the way he relates to people, and the new nature of a child of God?

As we follow Jesus and experience his patience with us and his kindness and goodness toward us, we learn to treat others in those same ways. As we become more and more secure in his love and confident that our lives are in his gentle, wise hands, we experience great and greater freedom in our dealings with people. We aren't "needy" when we rub shoulders with others. This liberates us to be generous, to help, and to bless. Suddenly we can overlook faults and let go of slights—both real and perceived. We can put up with the quirks and flaws of others. Rather than seeking to get even, we can resolve to bless.

> The fruit of the Spirit aren't just graces to receive or virtues to study, but qualities to practice.

Such relationships are possible only as we allow the Holy Spirit to control us (Galatians 5:22–23). Apart from such power, they are impossible.

Take-Home Reflections

Relational Role Play

Good intentions aren't enough in hard situations. *Planning* to be patient, kind, and good in your dealings with others is fine. But when others are harsh and situations are tense, the best plans can disappear like your breath on a cold morning. Don't just plan—practice. By yourself or with a friend, think through, talk through, or better yet, role play how you could respond in a Christ-like way in each of the everyday scenarios below.

Real-life Situation	My instinctive, natural reaction	A better response
A family member is about to make you late for an event that's very important to you.		
A coworker, obviously upset about something else, is taking it out on you.		
One rainy day after work, you see your supervisor—not a nice person—in the parking lot with the hood of his car up.		
You find out your "ex" made a really nasty comment about you on Facebook.		
You are still sitting and waiting in the doctor's lobby an hour and a half past your appointment time.		
A single mom has asked if you would watch her children for a couple of hours—but you really don't enjoy kids.		
The neighbors blare loud music all hours of the night, even after you politely asked them to tone it down due to your new baby.		

Life Application

An important part of discipleship is learning how to apply God's truths to your life. Below are just a few ways you can start thinking about what you've learned and apply it to your daily life.

1. Memorize our memory verse Galatians 5:22–23, NASB.

   "The fruit of the Spirit is love, joy, peace, forbearance, kindness, goodness, faithfulness, gentleness and self-control. Against such things there is no law."

2. Wrestle with one or two of these questions:

   ▷ It's been suggested that in the same way we only get better at a thing—running, weight lifting, etc.—by training to do that thing, the only way we'll ever get better at patience is by purposely putting ourselves in situations that will force us to slow down and/or deal with frustrating people. Advocates of this approach suggest picking the longest line at the bank drive-thru window, or resisting the urge to avoid that annoying person at work. What are the pros and cons of taking such a direct approach to learning patience?

   ▷ Two common proverbs champion the idea of patience: "Good things take time" and "Good things come to those who wait." When have you seen these proverbs prove to be true in your own life?

   ▷ This week, what's a specific act of kindness you could show to someone in your life who maybe doesn't "deserve" it? Write it down in the space below.

Topic 5: Faithfulness & Gentleness
Becoming God's Humble Servant

*"Take my yoke upon you and learn from
me, for I am gentle and humble in heart,
and you will find rest for your souls."*
—Matthew 11:29

**We become like those with
whom we associate.**

This is one of the great truisms of life.
Friends tend to pick up each other's speech
habits. Roommates mimic one another's
mannerisms. Couples begin to think alike
and sometimes even to look alike!

In other words, it's not just adolescents
who battle peer pressure. All of us are
susceptible to the influence of others. This
is why the Bible warns us to avoid bad
company (1 Corinthians 15:33) and to "walk
with the wise" (Proverbs 13:20). This does
not mean that we avoid unbelievers (many

are good citizens), but we avoid people
who get us into trouble.

For followers of Christ, this truism is
fantastic news. It means by spending time
with Jesus, we really can become *like*
Jesus. In Galatians 5:22–23 we are given a
snapshot of the heart of Jesus, an example
of the way he lived.

In this lesson, we want to examine the
virtues of *faithfulness* and *gentleness*. What
are these qualities, and what do they look
like in a disciple's life?

Bible Study

Faithfulness

One of the traits that Paul says marks Spirit-filled followers of Christ is faithfulness. The Greek word is *pistis*, which is almost always translated "faith," though it can be rendered "faithfulness." It conveys confidence, certainty, or trust. To have faith is to have those things; to be faithful is to inspire such things in others.

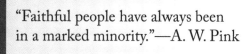

"Faithful people have always been in a marked minority."—A. W. Pink

Ponder these verses that highlight the faithfulness of our God:

▶ "Because of the Lord's great love we are not consumed, for his compassions never fail. They are new every morning; great is your faithfulness" (Lamentations 3:22–24).

▶ "But Christ is faithful as the Son over God's house. And we are his house, if indeed we hold firmly to our confidence and the hope in which we glory" (Hebrews 3:6).

▶ "If we are faithless, [Jesus] remains faithful—for he cannot deny himself" (2 Timothy 2:13, ESV).

1. Having pondered these verses, how would you describe faithfulness?

_____

_____

_____

In everyday terms, to be faithful means to be dependable. It means to be trustworthy, loyal, and consistent. A faithful person is reliable. You can count on him or her. If you are faithful, it means you will be there. You'll show up. You'll do what you said. You'll keep your promises—even when you're tired, or don't feel like it.

2. Describe a time in your life when you were blessed by God's faithfulness.

_____

_____

_____

_____

The Difference Faithfulness Makes

When a person is faithful—literally "full of faith"—it leads to a radically different life!

Expressions of Faith	→	Faithful Actions
"I was made by God—for his glory."	→	"I refuse to live today as if life is all about me."
"I am called and sent by God."	→	"I will seek my place in God's kingdom."
"I am uniquely blessed and gifted by God."	→	"I will use all that God has given me to serve and to bless others."
"God has promised to meet all of my needs in Christ Jesus."	→	"This frees me up to move toward others and meet their needs."
"Jesus has called me to be his disciple—to follow him and become like him."	→	"I will serve others, pouring out my life as Jesus served and poured out his life."
"Jesus is Lord of heaven and Earth—I will stand before him one day and give an account for how I have lived."	→	"I will live this day, with that day in view."

Gentleness

3. How would you define the word "gentleness"? What words or images come to mind when you think of someone who is gentle?

_____

_____

_____

The Greek word for "gentleness" is *prautes*. It was used in ancient times to refer to a *tame* beast, a *pleasant* person, or a *lenient* punishment. When this word gets translated as "meek," it is wrongly understood by some to suggest weakness or wimpiness—being soft or a pushover or a doormat. This is *not* the biblical idea.

"Jesus made this absolutely plain. The chief characteristic of Christian leaders . . . is humility not authority, and gentleness not power."
—John Stott

A tamed circus elephant is enormously powerful, but its strength is under control as it gently goes through its paces. Biblical gentleness is the same way. Instead of "powering up" in tense situations and "going off" on people when they do irresponsible things, gentle people allow the Spirit of God to pervade their lives. They are calm, humble, non-threatening—the very opposite of harsh or irritated. Instead of the power of pride and anger, a gentle disciple of Jesus opts for the power of humility. And as Proverbs 15:1 indicates, anger is no match for gentleness and humility!

Consider how the prophet Isaiah described God's Servant, the Messiah—Jesus—who would one day come: "A bruised reed he will not break, and a smoldering wick he will not snuff out. In faithfulness he will bring forth justice" (Isaiah 42:3).

4. When in your life have you been most touched by the gentleness of Christ? What were the circumstances? What happened?

For a great snapshot of faithfulness and gentleness in action, we need look no further than the actions of Christ on the night he was betrayed.

▷ He gathered together with his disciples—despite knowing that before the night was through, they would all betray, deny and/or desert him. Nevertheless, he was faithful to them and gentle with them. He tenderly washed their feet. He earnestly taught them important truths. He passionately prayed for them.

▷ And he wasn't only faithful to his followers. In his prayer he mentioned his utter faithfulness to the task God had given him to do (John 17:4).

▷ Later, in the Garden of Gethsemane, even when he was grieved by the terrible reality of what awaited him, he reiterated his desire to be faithful to the Father's will (Luke 22:42).

▷ Then, when violence broke out and one of those who had come to arrest him suffered a wound, Jesus gently touched the man and healed him (Luke 22:51).

What humility! What a servant! No one ever faced greater pressure or stress than Christ did on that night. And yet, he responded to every situation and every person with absolute faithfulness and gentleness.

What's your takeaway from this session? On a separate sheet of paper, journal your thoughts, perhaps even a prayer.

Take-Home Reflections

The following time-tested practice is called by different names. Bill Bright, the founder of Campus Crusade for Christ (now Cru) called it "spiritual breathing."

Essentially, it is taking a few moments to get alone in God's presence. If you find your heart and mind don't want to calm down, ask the Lord for internal peace.

▷ Breathe deeply. Recognize that God is with you and in you. Remember that he is gracious and kind. Through Christ, God is your heavenly father who cares for you. Trust his love.

▷ Ask him to show you any attitudes or actions that are inconsistent with a life lived in God. So, for example, as God points out your worry over a situation beyond your control—your fear over finances or health, a critical spirit toward someone, harshness toward your children—release these things into God's grace and care.

▷ Don't be in a rush. Linger in God's presence. Don't self-diagnose. Let God reveal. When he identifies things that are making your soul sick, respond in humility. Don't resist. Agree with God, and accept his forgiveness. This is really what "confession" is (see 1 John 1:9).

▷ Express your desire to be rid of everything toxic, to live in freedom, and to repent—to change your thinking and behavior about unhealthy things. Then ask to receive the blessings that God wants to give you.

Life Application

An important part of discipleship is learning how to apply God's truths to your life. Below are just a few ways you can start thinking about what you've learned and apply it to your daily life.

1. Memorize our verse, Matthew 11:29.

2. In one sitting, read John 13–21. Put yourself in the narrative. Pretend you are there with the twelve disciples. Watch Jesus. Pay close attention to his words. Notice his humility—how he serves faithfully and gently.

3. Wrestle with one or two of the following:

   ▷ Can you think of some ways in which you think, talk, act, look, and dress like other people with whom you spend a lot of time? What other characteristics might you be picking up from them?

   ▷ Who are some of the people in your life you'd classify as "gentle"? What specifically do they do or not do to warrant this description?

   ▷ What are some specific areas of your life in which you could stand to be more faithful—either from God's point of view or toward other people?

   ▷ We all have "pet peeves"—things that tend to get under our skin, and cause us to react strongly instead of gently and humbly. What are some of your pet peeves? How do you handle them?

Topic 6: Self-Control

Keeping It All in Check

"Like a city whose walls are broken through
is a person who lacks self-control."
—Proverbs 25:28

How Much Self-Control Do You Have?

Let's start with a quick personal assessment. For each of the following situations, on a typical day, what are the chances that you would respond in a God-honoring, people-blessing, soul-enhancing way? Place an X underneath the appropriate percentage.

Situation	0%	25%	50%	75%	100%
You're trying to lose weight, but a friend is serving her famous "Death by Chocolate" dessert. You want to resist, but it is the most delicious thing you ever put in your mouth.					
You've been wanting to get up thirty minutes earlier so you can start the habit of reading the Bible before work. But now the alarm is going off . . . and it's so early . . . and ten more minutes of sleep would be awesome.					
On the way home from work, an accident on the expressway causes a delay. As you creep along the guy behind you lays on his horn and gestures wildly at you when you let someone merge over in front of you.					
As you're bringing bags and bags of expensive groceries into the kitchen, your surly, ungrateful teenager complains that you forgot to get a new box of Choco-Carb Clusters cereal.					
On Facebook, someone posts a completely ridiculous video of the political candidate you can't stand, and the candidate is saying something totally outrageous.					
In the most crucial moment of the most important game of the season, the umpire makes a terrible call against your child.					
You walk into the living room to discover that your toddler has "finger-painted" the sofa with the contents of his diaper.					

Situation	0%	25%	50%	75%	100%
The hotel you're staying in (alone) has complimentary premium channels. The movie line-up features several NC-17 films.					
You discover that back-stabbing coworker who is always throwing people under the bus has made a huge mistake and is blaming you.					
It's 4:42 in the afternoon and while prepping for that important business meeting at 8:00 the next morning, you realize the report contains the wrong numbers. And even if you could correct it, the copy machine is on the fritz.					

According to the New Testament, a Christian disciple is a person who follows Jesus for three reasons:

▶ To *know* Jesus and his teaching

▶ To *grow* more like Jesus

▶ To *go* for Jesus, serving and making new disciples.

Bible Study

Disciples who grow to be more like Jesus take on his character. One important aspect of Christ-likeness is having and demonstrating *self-control*.

1. How would you define and describe the quality or attribute of self-control?

_____

_____

_____

_____

This virtue is listed as one of the nine "fruit of the Spirit" in Galatians 5:22–23. The Greek word translated "self-control" there is *enkrateia*. It speaks of corralling one's emotional impulses, bridling ones' appetites or passions, and resisting temptation. The result is a person who is purposeful and in harmony with the will of God.

A self-controlled man is wisely restrained, not wildly reactive. A self-controlled woman is intentional, not impulsive. When we are self-controlled we refrain from indulging our momentary selfish whims. Instead we choose actions that will result in long-term joy.

2. Read the following passage from the Bible:

"When [Jesus' accusers] hurled their insults at him, he did not retaliate; when he suffered, he made no threats. Instead, he entrusted himself to him who judges justly" (1 Peter 2:23).

How did Jesus demonstrate self-control? What might he have done instead?

_____

_____

_____

_____

_____

3. Read the following passage from the Bible:

"Do you not know that those who run in a race all run, but only one receives the prize? Run in such a way that you may win. Everyone who competes in the games exercises self-control in all things. They then do it to receive a perishable wreath, but we an imperishable. Therefore I run in such a way, as not without aim; I box in such a way, as not beating the air; but I discipline my body and make it my slave, so that, after I have preached to others, I myself will not be disqualified." (1 Corinthians 9:24–27, NASB)

a. Paul refers to runners and athletes. What can they teach us about self-control?

_____

_____

_____

_____

b. What would you say if someone said, "Self-control is just another word for willpower"?

_____

_____

_____

_____

The teaching of the New Testament is that we have more "will-weakness" than willpower. The gospel shows us that self-control doesn't come from a hardened resolve. It comes from a humbled heart. Rather than steeling our wills . . . we need to surrender them. Instead of grabbing the steering wheel of our lives, we give the wheel to another—to the Holy Spirit.

No book of the Bible illustrates this better than the Apostle Paul's letter to the church at Ephesus, the book of Ephesians. These six short chapters are a masterpiece of theological writing, a beautiful summary of the Christian life.

> ▶ In chapters 1–3, Paul doesn't tell Christians to *do* anything; instead, he gushes about all the amazing things God has done for us in Christ.

> ▶ In chapters 4–6 Paul shows how all those spiritual blessings make a difference in the way we live from day-to-day. He rattles off thirty-five specific commands for how we should be interacting in the home, in the church, and in the world.

> Ironically, we find self-control only when we relinquish control of ourselves to another.

Reading this divine "to do" list for Christians in Ephesians 4–6 can be intimidating—unless and until you pay close attention to Ephesians 5:18. That verse commands, "Don't be drunk with wine, because that will ruin your life. Instead, be filled with the Holy Spirit" (NLT).

4. Why do you think Paul compared and contrasted life in the Spirit with drunkenness?

_____

_____

_____

_____

Anyone who's ever had too much to drink knows the controlling power of alcohol. It takes over a person's personality—the inhibited person becomes outgoing, the frustrated person wants to pick a fight, the stoic person becomes sentimental. Though it's always wrong to *drive* under the influence of alcohol, it's always right to *live* under the influence of the Spirit (Galatians 5:16–18)!

It's worth noting that this command is in the present tense. That means it's to be an ongoing, never-ending reality. Being filled with or under the influence of God's Spirit is to be the moment-by-moment way of life for a disciple.

Also, the verb Paul uses in Ephesians 5:18 is passive. In other words, being filled with the Holy Spirit isn't something we make happen; it is something that happens *to us*. God does it—but only when we desire his control and open ourselves up to his guiding, transforming presence.

Important Points to Remember

▷ If you're a Christian, God's Spirit lives in you (Romans 8:9)—whether you "feel" him or not. As someone once quipped, "He's *resident* in you—even if you're not allowing Him to be *president* of you." This means Christians don't need to "receive the Spirit"—we need to unleash the Spirit.

▷ We can't be *filled* with the Spirit when we are *grieving* the Spirit (Ephesians 4:30) or *quenching* the Spirit (1 Thessalonians 5:19). Being filled with the Spirit is a way of saying we are surrendering to his control and allowing him to lead us (Romans 8:14).

▷ There's no secret prayer for "being filled with God's Spirit." It requires acknowledging and confessing any wrong attitudes or actions so that you will be a clean vessel, useful to the Lord (see 1 John 1:9; 2 Timothy 2:21). Jesus said the Spirit would be like a river within us (John 7:38–39). Not letting the Spirit fill us is like damming up that "holy river." However, when we confess known sin we "blow up the dam." After confession comes expression, telling God about our desire to have his Spirit rule in our hearts and minds and lives.

Every day—and all through each day—we must choose:

▷ Will I yield control of my life to the indwelling Spirit of God?

▷ Or will I try to power through situations in my own strength?

Those who have tried human willpower know the futility of such an approach. You may be able to resist temptation for a time, but wrong impulses and fleshly desires are like the waves at the beach. They keep coming at you relentlessly.

> "Self-control is not control by oneself through one's own willpower but rather control of oneself through the power of the Holy Spirit." —Jerry Bridges

The disciple realizes *Though I cannot truly control my behavior, I can control who controls my behavior.* Biblical self-control is choosing to say "no!" to the flesh, our old fallen human nature, and surrendering control instead to the Holy Spirit.

A disciple of Jesus allows the Spirit of God to fill him or her. This means listening to his promptings, soliciting his guidance, relying on his power. The fruit of such a life is divine strength—being able to resist sin, confess when we fail, get up again, and carry out God's will.

Verbal Self-Control

Consider these insights from the book of Proverbs, written by Solomon. Each one reinforces our need for spiritual power in restraining our tongue.

- ▶ "Sin is not ended by multiplying words, but the prudent hold their tongues" (10:19).

- ▶ "The lips of the righteous know what finds favor, but the mouth of the wicked only what is perverse" (10:32).

- ▶ "With their mouths the godless destroy their neighbors, but through knowledge the righteous escape" (11:9).

- ▶ "The words of the reckless pierce like swords, but the tongue of the wise brings healing" (12:18).

- ▶ "The LORD detests lying lips, but he delights in people who are trustworthy" (12:22).

- ▶ "Those who guard their lips preserve their lives, but those who speak rashly will come to ruin" (13:3).

- ▶ "The hearts of the wise make their mouths prudent, and their lips promote instruction" (16:23).

- ▶ "Gracious words are a honeycomb, sweet to the soul and healing to the bones" (16:24).

- ▶ "Even fools are thought wise if they keep silent, and discerning if they hold their tongues" (17:28).

- ▶ "Those who guard their mouths and their tongues keep themselves from calamity" (21:23).

- ▶ "A lying tongue hates those it hurts, and a flattering mouth works ruin" (26:28).

- ▶ "Do you see someone who speaks in haste? There is more hope for a fool than for them" (29:20).

Take-Home Reflections

Consider Your Speech Habits

Take some time to prayerfully, honestly consider the content of your recent conversations, your verbal interactions and writings (Facebook posts, Tweets, etc.). What do you find? On which side of the table do you find yourself most of the time? What do you need to do?

Sinful Speech Habits	or	Holy Speech Habits?
False teaching—advocating unbiblical ideas	—	Declaring God's truth with holy fear and trembling
Grumbling and complaining	—	Expressing gratitude and appreciation
Criticizing, critiquing, or fault-finding	—	Praying: "Show me the log in my eye." (Matthew 7:5)
Bragging, boasting, or taunting	—	Humility in speech
Flattery or insincere speech	—	Speaking the truth in love
Avoiding hard but necessary conversations	—	Confronting with tenderness and genuine concern
Slander, gossip, or backstabbing	—	Talking to others, rather than about them
Exaggerating or misrepresenting	—	Speaking accurately and with integrity
Lying—including shading the truth; telling half-truths, lies of omission, etc.	—	Truth-telling—no misleading, no matter what
Enticing or inciting others to evil	—	Exhorting others to holiness
Blaming others	—	Naming, owning, admitting, and confessing all of my faults
Blasphemy	—	Praising God in words, hymns, and songs
Snide, rude, or insensitive comments	—	Verbal kindness, honor, courtesy, and respect
Belittling, insulting, or cutting remarks	—	Speech that encourages, builds up, strengthens
Verbal abuse	—	Choosing and using words that bring healing and give life
Idle, careless, silly, or worldly speech	—	Sharing the gospel; discussing eternal realities
Cursing or profanity	—	Talking about what is good, beautiful, and noble

Sinful Speech Habits	or	Holy Speech Habits?
Negativity or pessimism	—	Expressing faith and hope in God's goodness and power
Arguing, bickering, or accusing	—	Seeking peace and pursuing conflict resolution
Expressing bitterness or rehashing old resentments against others	—	Extending and requesting forgiveness
Shaming or "guilting" others with words	—	Blessing others with words of grace and mercy
Heated conversations about God with skeptics and unbelievers	—	Gently giving a reason for the hope within you; using loving words
Talking incessantly	—	Silence

Life Application

An important part of discipleship is learning how to apply God's truths to your life. Below are just a few ways you can start thinking about what you've learned and apply it to your daily life.

1. Memorize our memory verse, Proverbs 25:28.

   "Like a city whose walls are broken through is a person who lacks self-control."

2. Read the Book of Ephesians in one sitting—from a translation you don't typically use.

3. Wrestle with one or two of these questions:

   ▶ What does our memory verse mean? Why the picture of a wall-less city?

   ▶ How would you respond to someone saying, "How can you say Jesus had self-control? He went through the temple with a whip, driving out the moneychangers, and turning over tables!"?

   ▶ What's the hardest thing about giving up control of your life?

   ▶ In the world of sports, we often hear about the importance of players or teams "buying in" to a coach's system, philosophy, or training regimen. In what ways is being filled with the Spirit like "buying in" to his leadership?

   ▶ If we rarely see the fruit of the Spirit in our lives (Galatians 5:22–23), is that a sure sign we are not allowing ourselves to be filled with the Spirit (Ephesians 5:18)?

Topic 7: Forgiveness

Being a Conduit of God's Mercy and Grace

"Bear with each other and forgive one another
if any of you has a grievance against someone.
Forgive as the Lord forgave you."
—Colossians 3:13

We live in a fallen, broken world. There's no way to avoid getting hurt—or hurting others. We collect scars even as we cause them. How then, is it possible for things like the following three examples to happen?

▶ Only days after a man opens fire in a church Bible study, killing nine innocent people, relatives of the victims attend a legal hearing to address the gunman. The teary first words of the very first speaker are, "I forgive you."

▶ A POW, who was sadistically abused while in captivity during World War II, longs to meet with the evilest of his guards, not to exact revenge, but to extend forgiveness.

▶ A mother befriends the young gang member who murdered her son and, when he finishes his prison sentence, unofficially adopts him.

Since, on any given day, we are both victims and perpetrators, we need to become experts at *forgiveness*.

Two things are true about a devoted follower of Jesus:

▶ He or she understands being *forgiven*.

▶ He or she understands being *forgiving*.

Bible Study

To learn about the concept of forgiveness, we could go to multiple places in the Bible. But perhaps one of the best passages is a story Jesus told. Take a moment to read the parable of the unmerciful servant from Matthew 18:21–35:

> Then Peter came to Jesus and asked, "Lord, how many times shall I forgive my brother or sister who sins against me? Up to seven times?"
>
> Jesus answered, "I tell you, not seven times, but seventy-seven times.
>
> "Therefore, the kingdom of heaven is like a king who wanted to settle accounts with his servants. As he began the settlement, a man who owed him ten thousand bags of gold was brought to him. Since he was not able to pay, the master ordered that he and his wife and his children and all that he had be sold to repay the debt.
>
> "At this the servant fell on his knees before him. 'Be patient with me,' he begged, 'and I will pay back everything.' The servant's master took pity on him, canceled the debt and let him go.
>
> "But when that servant went out, he found one of his fellow servants who owed him a hundred silver coins. He grabbed him and began to choke him. 'Pay back what you owe me!' he demanded.
>
> "His fellow servant fell to his knees and begged him, 'Be patient with me, and I will pay it back.' "But he refused. Instead, he went off and had the man thrown into prison until he could pay the debt. When the other servants saw what had happened, they were outraged and went and told their master everything that had happened.
>
> "Then the master called the servant in. 'You wicked servant,' he said, 'I canceled all that debt of yours because you begged me to. Shouldn't you have had mercy on your fellow servant just as I had on you?' In anger his master handed him over to the jailers to be tortured, until he should pay back all he owed.
>
> "This is how my heavenly Father will treat each of you unless you forgive your brother or sister from your heart."

1. Jesus told this story when Peter asked a question about *forgiveness*.

    a. How would you explain forgiveness to a child?

    _____

    _____

    _____

The Meaning of Forgiveness

The Greek word, *aphesis*, translated "to forgive," means to pardon, or to remove guilt. This gracious act doesn't erase the wrong act itself or take away the consequences of hurtful words and bad behaviors; however, it does effectively remove the wrongdoer's *guilt* and our own need to *get revenge*.

The other primary New Testament verb translated "forgive" (Luke 7:42–43; Ephesians 4:32) is *charizomai*. It means to graciously and generously cancel a debt.

The Mechanics of Forgiveness

Consider Matthew 6:15, "If you do not forgive others their sins, your Father will not forgive your sins."

To understand this verse and the concept of forgiveness more fully, let's dig into one of Jesus' parables. Take the time to read it now, Matthew 18:21–35.

In this parable Jesus is teaching us about sin and forgiveness. It is not difficult to tell who the characters are intended to represent. The king or master is representative of God. The servant represents an average person.

b. In the parable, what was the plea of the man heavily in debt (vs. 26)?

_____

_____

_____

The man's proposal is both ridiculous and sad. One scholar claims that a single silver talent represented 6,000 days' worth of wages for an average Palestinian worker (that's twenty-seven years of work!). So, ten thousand talents would be the equivalent of sixty million days' wages (working for 164,383.5 years). And that's if we're talking about talents of *silver*. It would be far more if Jesus meant talents of *gold*!

c. What's Jesus' point? What debt do we owe God because of our failure to properly love and honor him?

_____

_____

_____

We are either naïve, ignorant, or prideful to think *we* can somehow erase the debt we owe God. Spiritually speaking, the truth is that we keep dishonoring God *and adding to our debt!* Jesus' point is that our debt to God is far greater than we could ever pay back or even comprehend.

d. Read verse 27 again. What does the master or the king do for the man?

_____

_____

_____

_____

e. Read Colossians 2:13–14. How—not in the parable, but in the real world—is God able to cancel the enormous spiritual debts of sinful people?

_____

_____

_____

_____

The man in the parable asked for time. "Be patient!" he cried. He got infinitely more than that. He got the slate wiped clean, a big, thick ledger book full of bills—all cancelled! The king purged the books, expunged the records. Can you imagine?

f. Summarize the rest of the story. What did the forgiven man do next?

Just before he died on the cross, Jesus cried out, *tetellesthai,* or "It is finished!" This word was found on first-century invoices or accounting ledgers. Its meaning? *Paid in full.*

PAID IN FULL

_____

_____

_____

_____

g. How did the king respond when he heard about what the forgiven man had done?

_____

_____

_____

2. Read Matthew 18:34–35 and James 2:13. What's the warning for those who have experienced God's forgiveness but are unwilling to extend such mercy to others?

_____

_____

_____

The "Messiness" of Forgiveness

All this talk about forgiveness raises a number of questions. Let's look at a few of them.

How are we supposed to forgive the "unforgiveable"?

3. How would you counsel a friend who has been the victim of a great betrayal, horrific abuse, or a criminal act resulting in tragic loss? What can we possibly say that doesn't seem glib, trite, or like a cliché?

_____

_____

_____

The word "resentment" comes from two Latin words: _re_ meaning "again" and _sentire_ meaning "to feel." Resenting someone is to relive over and over again the pain or hurt they caused. In a real sense it is to be tortured by the pain of bitterness and unforgiveness.

What about vengeance? Isn't forgiveness unfair?

4. Read Hebrews 10:30 and Romans 12:19. What do these verses say about divine justice?

_____

_____

_____

What if I have lingering negative feelings?

For instance, sometimes I think about the person who hurt me and I start to feel angry or weird all over again. Does that mean I haven't forgiven?

5. Read three passages from Philippians: 1:6; 2:12–13; 3:12–16. How do these verses suggest that forgiveness might be

> All too often we lose sight of how lavishly God has forgiven our wrongs, and we focus instead on how others have violated our rights.

   a. A decision:

   _____

   _____

   _____

   b. An event:

   _____

   _____

   _____

   c. And an ongoing process?

   _____

   _____

   _____

What about the person who continues to cause me harm?

6. Read 1 Corinthians 5, NLT. What does this passage say about putting up boundaries? Note the reference to abusive people in verse 11.

   _____

   _____

   _____

Loving and forgiving our enemies means seeing them as fellow human beings who are loved by God and in need of his mercy and grace. The Bible *never* suggests that forgiving others—especially those who continue to act in hurtful ways—means tolerating abuse or subjecting yourself to ongoing physical or emotional danger. That isn't love; it's a kind of masochism. It isn't helpful or honorable; it's dysfunctional.

What about reconciliation and restoration?

7. Read 1 Thessalonians 5:11 and Romans 12:10. What do these verses suggest about restoring relationships after one or both parties have engaged in hurtful actions?

Forgiveness is not the same thing as reconciliation. Forgiveness means to pardon others, to no longer demand payment for their sins. Reconciliation is "restoration to harmony in relationship." With God, such restoration is always possible; but with humans it's tricky. Forgiveness is required, but the person who is forgiven may not change or become more trustworthy. In some instances, one person may not want to remain bitter, but he or she also may not wish to resume a relationship like before.

We can take the initiative to release people from their moral debts and still not enjoy reconciliation and restoration. Those blessings require repentance, confession on the part of the offender, and sometimes, restitution.

Take-Home Reflections

From Jesus' parable of the unforgiving servant, we see that

To be unwilling to forgive is to . . .	To forgive is to . . .
Disobey God's command (Colossians 3:13)	Learn what it means to trust God deeply
Ignore the infinite mercy God has shown us	Incarnate the Gospel
Experience the tortuous effects of bitterness	Vanquish the power of evil (Romans 12:21)
	Experience freedom and peace
Refusing to forgive is lethal!	**Choosing to forgive is life-giving!**

Forgiveness is the only path to the abundant life Jesus offers. The unwillingness to forgive is a kind of living death. Disciples of Jesus are marked by a forgiving spirit.

Life Application

An important part of discipleship is learning how to apply God's truths to your life. Below are just a few ways you can start thinking about what you've learned and apply it to your daily life.

1. Memorize our verse, Colossians 3:13.

2. Read one or two of the stories in the chart "Bible Stories of Forgiveness."

3. Wrestle with one or two of the following:

   ▶ Is it possible to "forgive and *forget*?" Is it necessary to forget?

   ▶ When we've wronged another, is it enough to simply ask God's forgiveness?

   ▶ Is there anyone you can think of from whom you need to ask forgiveness?

   ▶ What person or people in your life do you need to forgive?

Bible Stories of Forgiveness

Story Title	Reference(s)
Jacob and Esau	Genesis 25, 27, 32, 33
Joseph Forgives His Brothers	Genesis 37—50
David and Mephibosheth	2 Samuel 9
Prodigal Son	Luke 15
Casting the First Stone	John 8

Topic 8: Overcoming

The Ongoing Battle with Sin and Temptation

"Fight the good fight of the faith. Take hold
of the eternal life to which you were called
when you made your good confession in
the presence of many witnesses."
—1 Timothy 6:12

In his book *Learning from the Giants*, John C. Maxwell observed that "Disappointment comes when reality falls short of our expectations." For example, you finally make reservations at that chic new bistro that everyone has been *raving* about. You're primed for stellar service and amazing French food—but for some reason, the chef and staff at Le Veau D'or have an off night. You leave majorly bummed out. Why?

Here's the truth, at one time or another, every Christian ends up *disappointed*. This is because we often get it in our heads that following Jesus is going to lead to a certain outcome . . . but then life, reality and/or God don't cooperate.

Let's examine this idea of spiritual disappointment—the common phenomenon of spiritual reality not living up to our spiritual expectations. And the struggle we all experience as a result of this disappointment.

Great Expectations

Put a check mark in the box for any of the following spiritual expectations you've had.

- ☐ If I humbly ask God to forgive my sins, he will.

- ☐ Turning to Jesus is the quickest, surest way to fix my problems—marital, financial, occupational, academic, social, medical, etc.

- ☐ God will always be with me, always love me, always approve of what I do.

- ☐ If I pray hard enough God might "zap me" and take away sinful desires or bad habits.

- ☐ If I tack the expression "in Jesus' name, amen" to the end of my prayers, God is obligated to give me whatever I've asked for.

- ☐ I should always expect to "sense" or "feel" God's presence in my life.

☐ A devoted Christian should never and will never get depressed.

☐ If I follow certain principles or parenting techniques my kids will never turn away from God.

☐ If I have enough faith I can enjoy a life of continual physical health and financial prosperity.

☐ The gospel and followers of Christ will always be honored in our culture.

☐ Here and now, I can have the experience of heaven—flawless people, including myself; perfect situations; everything and everyone unaffected by sin; etc.

☐ There are certain sins that I would *never* commit.

☐ In many aspects, following Jesus will actually make my life harder and more complicated.

☐ I can mature in my faith, in this life, to the point that I will no longer be tempted by certain sins.

☐ It's possible to arrive at a place in this life where I have constant peace, unending bliss, and unshakeable faith all day, every day.

☐ I can be wholeheartedly devoted to Christ and be liked and admired and accepted by everyone.

☐ The spiritual life is going to be an exhausting race and a brutal battle.

For each box you checked, ask yourself these questions:

▶ Why do I expect this to be true in my experience?

▶ What passage(s) in the Bible tells me I should expect this?

▶ Has this expectation always been true in my experience?

Bible Study

Listen to the confessions of three very different Christians:

▶ "My upbringing was totally dysfunctional. I was the only child of a single mom with drug and alcohol issues. By the time I graduated high school, my mom had been married four times to three different guys! In between, she had five or six live-in boyfriends. We moved about every six months. It was constant drama. So when I heard the gospel as a teenager, all that talk of "new life" and "being saved," I jumped at it. For sure, my life changed. But if I'm honest, there's still a lot of drama in my life, and it's not even my mom now. I look at some of the ways I act and think *I am so screwed up! Shouldn't I be different?*"—Savannah, 23, grad student

▶ "For as long as I can remember, two things have been true. One, I have always loved God and tried to follow Christ. And, two, I've been attracted to guys. I never consciously chose that. It just is. Over the last 20 years, I bet I've prayed 10,000 times, 'God, if I'm not supposed to have these urges, would you please . . . *please* . . . take them away?' He hasn't. You tell me: Why wouldn't God answer that prayer?"—Karl, 33, accountant

▶ "For the first six or seven years after divinity school, being a pastor was really gratifying. Then it slowly became grueling. I felt like all around me people were drowning, and meanwhile I was barely keeping my own head above the waterline. I never thought serving God and serving people would be so hard."—Walter, 49, ex-minister

1. What words or phrases would you use to describe what these three are feeling?

_____

_____

_____

_____

_____

2. In what ways do you relate to their disappointment or disillusionment?

_____

_____

_____

_____

_____

3. What are the biggest disappointments you've experienced so far with God, the spiritual life, or following Christ?

_____

_____

_____

_____

_____

Spiritual Reality According to the Bible

Take a few minutes to read, ponder, and write a response to these nine Scripture passages that discuss and/or describe the experience of being a follower of Christ. The first one has been filled out as an example.

The passage	What it reveals about struggle	My reality
"Let us not become weary in doing good, for at the proper time we will reap a harvest if we do not give up." (Galatians 6:9)	*Doing good can wear you out and make you feel like giving up, but there's a reward if we hang in there!*	*Volunteering in kids' ministry is tough. I feel like quitting some weeks, but I know it's worth it!*
"Let us not become weary in doing good, for at the proper time we will reap a harvest if we do not give up." (Galatians 6:9)		
"For I do not do the good I want to do, but the evil I do not want to do—this I keep on doing." (Romans 7:19)		
"Not only that, but we rejoice in our sufferings, knowing that suffering produces endurance, and endurance produces character, and character produces hope." (Romans 5:3–4, ESV)		
"Indeed, all who desire to live a godly life in Christ Jesus will be persecuted." (2 Timothy 3:12, ESV)		
"The temptations in your life are no different from what others experience. And God is faithful. He will not allow the temptation to be more than you can stand. When you are tempted, he will show you a way out so that you can endure." (1 Corinthians 10:13, NLT)		
"For our struggle is not against flesh and blood, but against the rulers, against the authorities, against the powers of this dark world and against the spiritual forces of evil in the heavenly realms." (Ephesians 6:12)		

The passage	What it reveals about struggle	My reality
"Be of sober spirit, be on the alert. Your adversary, the devil, prowls around like a roaring lion, seeking someone to devour." (1 Peter 5:8, NASB)		
"Here on earth you will have many trials and sorrows. But take heart, because I have overcome the world." (John 16:33, NLT)		
"Dear friends, I urge you, as foreigners and exiles, to abstain from sinful desires, which wage war against your soul." (1 Peter 2:11)		

4. What are your big takeaways from this exercise? How do these verses describe the spiritual reality of a follower of Jesus?

_____

_____

_____

We speak often of becoming *disillusioned*—and we say that like it's a bad thing. But consider for a moment what that word really means. The prefix *dis* means "apart, away, or without," so to be *disillusioned* is literally to be "without illusions." It means to be pulled away from what we only *thought* was real and true! Disillusionment is actually *the process of coming back to reality*. That may not be fun. But it's vital and good.

What's the reality of the spiritual life, of following Jesus?

When we read the Scripture, we often spin it by

▶ Forcing the Bible to say things it doesn't say

▶ Ignoring its clear but dark truths

However, if we *don't* spin Scripture, we would likely come to the following conclusions:

▶ Life is hard. And faith in Christ doesn't promise to make things easy. In fact, following Jesus means we can expect the world to hate us, the enemy of our souls to assault us, and our unredeemed human nature to fiercely resist God's transforming work within us. We can and should expect an epic struggle because the spiritual life is a fight. We live in a world at war.

We can expect to grow spiritually, but never arrive at perfection this side of heaven. We will face powerful temptations up until the day we die. We will resist them sometimes, and we will cave in lots of other times. Not even our worst failures will alter God's love for us.

Even though we are God's beloved children, we should expect to face trials—lots of little ones and others that are big and terrifying. No Christian gets a pass from suffering. The Scripture doesn't guarantee anyone a disease-free or accident-free life. On the contrary, the Bible says life will have its bitter moments and its glorious ones too. And the history of God's people shows this to be true. When the pain doesn't take our breath

> "How often we look upon God as our last and feeblest resource. We go to him because we have nowhere else to go. And then we learn that the storms of life have driven us, not upon the rocks, but into the desired haven."—George MacDonald

away, the beauty just might. We will cry a lot. And we will do our share of laughing too.

> "Your life is not going to be easy, and it should not be easy. It ought to be hard. It ought to be radical; it ought to be restless; it ought to lead you to places you'd rather not go."
> —Henri Nouwen

We could go on and on:

- How we won't understand many things.

- How many of our prayers won't be answered in ways we'd like.

- How serving others will be exhausting, and how some will never acknowledge our sacrifice, and others will actually grumble at our efforts.

We will want to quit again and again, which is why we need to follow Jesus with others alongside to encourage us.

Understanding these things is how we become healthily disillusioned about the spiritual life. These are the realities we should expect.

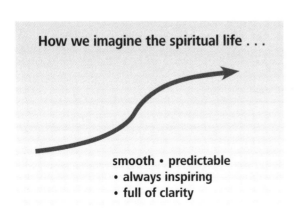

How we imagine the spiritual life . . .

smooth • predictable
• always inspiring
• full of clarity

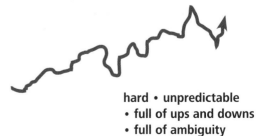

What the spiritual life is really like . . .

hard • unpredictable
• full of ups and downs
• full of ambiguity

Take-Home Reflections

C. S. Lewis' ingenious book, *The Screwtape Letters* tells the tale of a crafty, mid-level devil giving advice to a less wily apprentice. Screwtape, the older demon, discusses the way God often gives new converts obvious reminders of his presence, warm spiritual feelings, and even a strong desire to turn away from temptation.

"But," Screwtape continues, "He never allows this state of affairs to last long. Sooner or later He withdraws, if not in fact, at least from their conscious experience, all those supports and incentives. He leaves the creature to stand up on its own legs—to carry out from the will alone duties which have lost all relish. It is during such trough periods, much more than during the peak periods, that it is growing into the sort of creature He wants it to be."

In other words, God allows his children to struggle. Struggle is a normal part of the spiritual life. Struggle is how we grow and make progress in the faith. If you are struggling in the faith, it's not a sign of failure. It's a sign you are on the path that all disciples are called to walk.

So keep walking. *And make sure you walk with other believers.* Discipleship is a hard battle and a holy journey, but we were never meant to fight or journey alone (Ecclesiastes 4:12).

If we don't give up, we will be able to say what the apostle Paul said just before his death, "I have fought the good fight, I have finished the race, I have kept the faith" (2 Timothy 4:7).

Life Application

An important part of discipleship is learning how to apply God's truths to your life. Below are just a few ways you can start thinking about what you've learned and apply it to your daily life.

1. Memorize our verse, 1 Timothy 6:12.

2. Read the sections from Paul's second letter to the Corinthians in which he describes his life as a devoted follower and servant of Jesus (2 Corinthians 6:4–10; 11:23–28). Why and how do you think Paul was able to endure such struggle?

3. Wrestle with one or two of the following:

   ▷ What were your expectations of God and of the spiritual life when you first came to faith?

   ▷ Have any of those expectations changed as you've grown spiritually?

   ▷ What has this lesson helped you see differently about following Jesus?

   ▷ What specific spiritual battles are most fierce in your life right now—fighting envy, lust, or doubt; trying to develop healthy spiritual habits, etc.?

Topic 9: Perseverance

Dealing with Doubts, Trials, and Fears

"Blessed is the one who perseveres under trial
because, having stood the test, that person
will receive the crown of life that the Lord has
promised to those who love him."

—James 1:12

It's tough to keep hanging in there when you're feeling doubts and facing problems, isn't it?

Maybe you're:

- A person with a lofty dream that is going to require grueling years of schooling—and even then you'll have no guarantees of success.

- Someone whose spouse is bitter and impossible to please.

- Caring for an aging parent with Alzheimer's or a child who requires around-the-clock care.

- A cancer patient who's facing another round of chemo with another drug because the last one was ineffective— just like the first two.

- The friendly kid at a new school who constantly gets teased, shunned and thinks, *What's the use? Why even try?*

- A laid-off worker who has sent out one hundred resumes without a single request for a follow-up interview.

Because life is tough—and sometimes brutal—lots of people quit things every day. They quit a job or walk away from a friendship. They give up on a dream or pull the plug on a marriage.

For anyone who is trying to follow Jesus, life's painful and persistent hardships can foster serious doubt. If you're struggling, you may even be asking questions like:

- Is God real?

- Why isn't this "faith in Christ thing" working?

- I thought Jesus came to make my life better and more blessed?

In this lesson, we want to look at the rare and wonderful quality of perseverance. Disciples have this trait because Jesus, the one they follow, had it. Why should you keep trusting the Father in heaven and walking with him, when doing so doesn't seem to make your life easier or better? In truth, in many places of the world, being a Christian makes your life exponentially *harder.* Is it really possible to "keep the faith" in a world filled with trouble?

Let's study perseverance and see how we can cultivate this noble virtue in our lives.

Bible Study

Perseverance: What Does It Mean?

In the New Testament, there are two primary Greek words that get translated "perseverance." One is *proskartere*. It means "to adhere" or "to cling" or "to be devoted." Some of our English Bibles translate it "to continue (in something)," "to be steadfast," or "to be constant."

Get this: In Mark 3:9, this word has been used of a boat that has been made ready for Jesus, devoted for his use, and sits waiting nearby. In Acts 10:7, it describes a faithful personal attendant. In short, the idea of perseverance is persisting, staying, waiting, not leaving—and doing all that when it's hard or boring, when you're being opposed, or whether or not you *feel* like it.

The other word is *hupomone*. It conveys the same ideas of endurance, patience, being steadfast, having to wait. Again, the implication is that you are weary of your hard circumstances, and tired of waiting for things to change. You want to throw in the towel. But the voice of perseverance urges, "Don't quit. Hang in there. Cling. Remain faithful despite the opposition and the tantalizing promises of life elsewhere."

In what specific ways are followers of Christ supposed to persevere?

Take a look at these verses that urge followers of Jesus to *persevere* in some aspect of the life of faith:

▷ "Be joyful in hope, patient in affliction, faithful in prayer" (Romans 12:12).

▷ "Let us not become weary in doing good, for at the proper time we will reap a harvest if we do not give up" (Galatians 6:9).

▷ "But you must remain faithful to the things you have been taught. You know they are true, for you know you can trust those who taught you" (2 Timothy 3:14, NLT).

▷ "Therefore, since we are surrounded by such a great cloud of witnesses, let us throw off everything that hinders and the sin that so easily entangles. And let us run with perseverance the race marked out for us" (Hebrews 12:1).

▶ "Be on guard. Stand firm in the faith. Be courageous. Be strong" (1 Corinthians 16:13, NLT).

▶ "Devote yourselves to prayer, being watchful and thankful" (Colossians 4:2).

▶ "And pray in the Spirit on all occasions with all kinds of prayers and requests. With this in mind, be alert and always keep on praying for all the Lord's people" (Ephesians 6:18).

▶ "So then, brothers and sisters, stand firm and hold fast to the teachings we passed on to you, whether by word of mouth or by letter" (2 Thessalonians 2:15).

1. This, of course, is only a partial listing of verses that call Christians to persevere, but what specific areas do you see mentioned?

2. How would you rate yourself when it comes to persevering in the areas just mentioned?

3. Read Hebrews 6:1–8 and 10:26–31. The New Testament includes a lot of warnings like these about falling away from faith. Here are a few other examples:

▶ "You will be hated by all because of My name, but it is the one who has endured to the end who will be saved." (Jesus, speaking in Matthew 10:22, NASB)

▶ "As God's coworkers we urge you not to receive God's grace in vain." (2 Cor. 6:1)

▶ "See to it, brothers and sisters, that none of you has a sinful, unbelieving heart that turns away from the living God." (Hebrews 3:12)

What do you make of these verses? What are they saying?

4. How would you describe the difference between a true believer who still sins and a "make believer" who never really had true faith and still sins?

_____

_____

_____

5. Check out these verses that speak of what God does to help disciples to persevere and remain faithful:

▷ "I give them eternal life, and they shall never perish; no one will snatch them out of my hand. My Father, who has given them to me, is greater than all; no one can snatch them out of my Father's hand" (Jesus, speaking in John 10:28–29).

▷ "God's gifts and his call are irrevocable" (Romans 11:29).

▷ "For I am confident of this very thing, that He who began a good work in you will perfect it until the day of Christ Jesus" (Philippians 1:6, NASB).

▷ "All praise to God, the Father of our Lord Jesus Christ. It is by his great mercy that we have been born again, because God raised Jesus Christ from the dead. Now we live with great expectation, and we have a priceless inheritance—an inheritance that is kept in heaven for you, pure and undefiled, beyond the reach of change and decay. And through your faith, God is protecting you by his power until you receive this salvation, which is ready to be revealed on the last day for all to see" (1 Peter 1:3–5, NLT).

What's That About?

I heard some Christians arguing about "the perseverance of the saints." They were wrestling with the question, "Can a believer lose his or her salvation?" or "Is it possible to have true faith and then turn away from it?" This is a hotly debated issue, but most Christians would agree with these statements:

• Some who claim to be believers are not truly born again due to misunderstanding of the gospel, insincerity, or misplaced trust, etc.

• God alone knows the truth about a person's heart and spiritual condition.

• Even redeemed people will continue to sin.

God is faithful to bring his children home. Those who have exercised genuine, saving faith—they've been made alive spiritually and declared righteous by virtue of Christ's death and resurrection on their behalf—cannot be un-adopted by God. Despite failure and sin, we cannot invalidate God's grace. He will faithfully see to it that we "persevere" and enter into everlasting life.

According to these verses, why—if we have faith in Christ—do we not have to fear?

_____

_____

_____

6. Writing to Christians who were facing a lot of hard things in life, the apostle James said:

"Consider it pure joy, my brothers and sisters, whenever you face trials of many kinds, because you know that the testing of your faith produces perseverance. Let perseverance finish its work so that you may be mature and complete, not lacking anything" (James 1:2–4).

Does that seem ridiculous to you? How is it possible to be joyful in hard times?

_____

_____

_____

Notice a couple of things. First, the passage says "whenever" and not "if by chance." In other words, trials are a fact of life. Disciples of Jesus don't get a pass from the troubles of this world. (You can study more about this truth in "Topic 19: Overcoming.")

Trials are never fun. But if we faithfully persevere, God brings good things out of our bad situations.

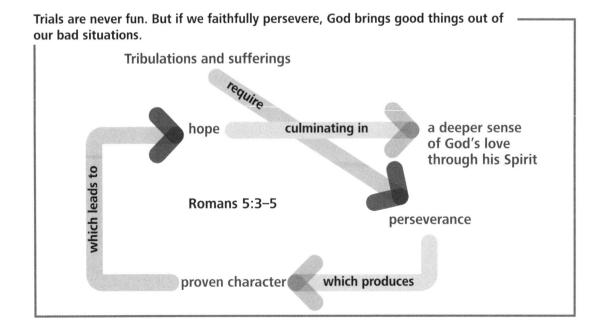

Tribulations and sufferings

require

hope — culminating in — a deeper sense of God's love through his Spirit

which leads to

Romans 5:3–5

perseverance

proven character ← which produces

Notice also that James says difficulties come our way not to ruin us, but to develop us and strengthen us. Trials are the God-ordained/God-orchestrated "laboratory" wherein we can develop perseverance. All that waiting, trusting, and clinging is how we come to know firsthand that we are tougher than we imagined, that we can endure more than we thought. And why? Because our God is more faithful than we ever dreamed.

What can we do to cultivate perseverance in our lives?

The Lord has given his children four great resources for the hard times of life:

1. **His Word.** "All Scripture is God-breathed and is useful for teaching, rebuking, correcting and training in righteousness, so that the servant of God may be thoroughly equipped for every good work" (2 Timothy 3:16–17).

   The trustworthy promises of the Bible can shore up our flagging faith.

2. **His Spirit.** "But the Advocate, the Holy Spirit, whom the Father will send in my name, will teach you all things and will remind you of everything I have said to you. Peace I leave with you; my peace I give you. I do not give to you as the world gives. Do not let your hearts be troubled and do not be afraid" (John 14:26–27).

   The indwelling Spirit can give us the power to continue to cling.

3. **His People.** "I thank my God every time I remember you. In all my prayers for all of you, I always pray with joy because of your partnership in the gospel from the first day until now" (Paul writing to the Philippians, from prison, 1:3–5).

   The body of Christ can surround us and provide encouragement to keep going.

4. **His Mission**. "But thanks be to God! He gives us the victory through our Lord Jesus Christ. Therefore, my dear brothers and sisters, stand firm. Let nothing move you. Always give yourselves fully to the work of the Lord, because you know that your labor in the Lord is not in vain" (1 Corinthians 15:57–58).

   Participation in an eternally worthy task can keep us focused on what matters.

> "Perseverance is . . . a call to faithfulness, but it is also an affirmation that somehow, in spite of our failures, God will bring His committed people through the difficulties and concerns of life to their promised destiny in Christ."
> —Gerald L. Borchert

What is perseverance? It is continuing to follow Jesus, even when he leads us to and through harrowing chapters of life. It is hanging on to and cultivating your faith through life's difficult times.

Ultimately, we are able to cling to God because he holds us firmly in his hands.

Take-Home Reflections

A Perseverance Self-Check

Check all the actions of perseverance you intend to live out.

By God's grace, secure in the love of Christ, and in the power of the Spirit:

- ☐ I will consistently open and read the Scripture, setting my hope on the things God says are true, and seeking to be a doer of the Word.

- ☐ I will be honest and authentic in prayer.

- ☐ I will, when I do, think, or say, wrong things, turn quickly to Jesus, who has forgiven me and who loves me unconditionally.

- ☐ I will honor my commitments—even when I don't feel like it.

- ☐ I will, by God's grace, step out in faith to do something that I feel is God's will but that makes me uncomfortable.

- ☐ I will seek to be faithful, not for the rest of my life, but in this moment.

- ☐ I will humble myself—confessing my sin, and asking forgiveness from those whom I have hurt.

- ☐ I will value and practice the disciplines of biblical community and spiritual friendship.

- ☐ I will initiate a much-needed conversation with a family member, friend, or coworker.

- ☐ I will cling desperately to God in my current trials—like a drowning person clinging to a lifeline.

Life Application

An important part of discipleship is learning how to apply God's truths to your life. Below are just a few ways you can start thinking about what you've learned and apply it to your daily life.

1. Memorize our memory verse, James 1:12.

   "Blessed is the one who perseveres under trial because, having stood the test, that person will receive the crown of life that the Lord has promised to those who love him."

2. Talk over the results of your Perseverance Self-Check with a trusted, confidential friend.

3. Share with the same friend or another, one of the current struggles in your life. Ask for prayer and encouragement as many struggles don't have easy answers, and some cannot be solved in this lifetime.

Topic 10: Discerning God's Will

Figuring Out What God Wants You to Do

"Do not conform to the pattern of this world,
but be transformed by the renewing of
your mind. Then you will be able to test
and approve what God's will is—
his good, pleasing and perfect will."
—Romans 12:2

Read the hypothetical situations described below. Try to identify what these three very different situations have in common.

▶ A new bestselling book by a well-known celebrity is creating a firestorm of controversy. Titled *Chruddism*, it offers a new kind of spirituality that blends the teachings of Christ with the tenets of Buddhism. Several of your Christian friends have read it, and say they loved it—that it opened up their eyes to some truths they'd never thought of before. What is your response?

▶ A bright high-school senior with test scores through the stratosphere has been offered full scholarships to three very different but equally prestigious colleges. There's much to commend each one. She likes them all, and is freaking out about which one is the best decision. What is your advice?

▶ You've been asked to help out with the shut-in ministry at your church. There is a huge need there, and you worked with senior citizens when you were in college. Part of you feels like this would be a good thing; another part of you just feels tired and frazzled. Your thoughts vacillate wildly between *I probably should do this* and *I already feel pulled in ten directions*. In the end, what is your response?

Did you figure out the common thread through all these examples? In each of the situations above, what's needed is *discernment*.

1. Name a situation in your life that causes you to struggle with what's right and true, or what may be the best course of action.

_____

_____

What Is Discernment?

Biblically speaking, discernment is the ability God's Spirit gives us to distinguish and decide between that which is true, wise, and good and that which is false, foolish, and evil.

God wants *all* of his children to have and exercise this ability. Consider these passages from the apostle Paul, written to the ancient Christians in Colossae and Philippi:

▶ "So, from the day we heard, we have not ceased to pray for you, asking that you may be filled with the knowledge of his will in all spiritual wisdom and understanding" (Colossians 1:9, ESV).

▶ "This is my prayer: that your love may abound more and more in knowledge and depth of insight, so that you may be able to discern what is best and may be pure and blameless for the day of Christ" (Philippians 1:9–10).

Bible Study

2. What does Paul request for Christians here? What ability does he want them to develop?

_____

_____

In 1 Corinthians 12, the apostle Paul discusses spiritual gifts—special God-given abilities for building up the body of Christ. Here we discover some Christians are given a special ability to discern between right and wrong, spiritual truth and spiritual error. It's like the Holy Spirit functions in their life like a built-in "bad theology detector."

"He gives one person the power to perform miracles, and another the ability to prophesy. He gives someone else the ability to discern whether a message is from the Spirit of God or from another spirit. Still another person is given the ability to speak in unknown languages, while another is given the ability to interpret what is being said." (1 Corinthians 12:10, NLT)

3. Do you know any Christians with this extra-special ability to correctly analyze situations and messages and say, "That's a bad idea" or "That works well with biblical teachings"? Give an example or two.

_____

_____

_____

What Is True, Wise, and Good

Here are four truths about figuring out what is true, wise, and good:

Truth #1: **God's will is discernible.**

Some believers act like God's will is accessible only to a few eccentric spiritual geniuses who have figured out how to "hack into the Almighty's heavenly database."

Not true. God is not trying to turn our lives into a frustrating search. We can discern his purposes for us. He *wants* us to know his will—so that we can do it!

4. Look at what our memory verse for this lesson tells us: "Do not conform to the pattern of this world, but be transformed by the renewing of your mind. Then you will be able to test and approve what God's will is—his good, pleasing and perfect will" (Romans 12:2).

How would you explain this verse to a child?

_____

_____

_____

Dangerous Assumptions About the Will of God

- He probably wants to send me to someplace miserable.
- I'll have to marry a boring, mean, or unattractive person. Or I'll never get married!
- He'll have me do something dreadful—something that I hate.
- His plans for my life won't be nearly as exciting as *my* plans for my life.
- I'll probably end up poor.
- Obeying God will take all the fun out of life.
- He'll make me suffer.
- His will likely involves a frustrating existence in a foreign country.

Clearly God desires for us to know his will today. He may not reveal his will for tomorrow, next month, or next year. But he gives us what we need to know now. We see this in the prayer of the Spirit-led psalmist: "Teach me to do Your will, for You are my God; let Your good Spirit lead me on level ground" (Psalm 143:10, NASB).

Truth #2: **God's will is good.**

Now we get to the heart of the issue. So many times Christians cringe at the phrase "the will of God," because they equate that with hard or bad things (see "Dangerous Assumptions About the Will of God"). We assume that if we seek hard after God's will, we just might find it, and that will involve all sorts of unpleasantness!

5. Consider the following passages:

- ▷ "For the LORD God is a sun and shield; the LORD bestows favor and honor; no good thing does he withhold from those whose walk is blameless" (Psalm 84:11).

- ▷ "Give thanks to the LORD, for he is good; his love endures forever" (Psalm 107:1).

- ▷ "'For I know the plans I have for you,' says the LORD. 'They are plans for good and not for disaster, to give you a future and a hope'" (Jeremiah 29:11, NLT).

- ▷ "He who did not spare his own Son, but gave him up for us all—how will he not also, along with him, graciously give us all things?" (Romans 8:32).

What conclusions might we draw from these passages about the will of God?

_____

_____

_____

_____

Someone has observed, if we really believed our heavenly Father's character is 100-percent good, every hour of every day, we'd trust his will, no matter what. And if we trusted his heart, we would *do* his will eagerly, as Jesus did (Matthew 26:42).

Here's what we have to believe: In following the way of Christ wholeheartedly, we find a life that simultaneously honors God, blesses others, and brings happiness to our own soul. Outside of embracing and doing the will of a good God, we will never find all of that.

6. Why is it a struggle for people to believe in God's love and care for us?

_____

_____

_____

_____

Truth #3: **Discerning God's will requires God's resources.**

These resources include God's Word, God's Spirit, as well as other resources.

God's Word

God doesn't give his children a detailed blueprint for life. Nobody gets a comprehensive itinerary for the next twenty, forty, or sixty years. Instead God gave us his Word.

What exactly is the Bible? Maybe we should start with what the Bible is not. It's not a day-planner. It's not going to give you explicit instructions for every situation of life—like whether you should wear your red shirt or your green one!

Rather, the Bible is the wild-but-true story of God. It's like a photograph album or scrapbook of sorts. It gives us glimpses and remembrances of what God is like and how he's acted in history. It's also a love letter full of divine promises. And further, it's a show-and-tell of the best and worst ways to live.

7. What would happen to our relationship with God if instead of the Bible, God gave each of his children a personalized app that dinged and buzzed moment-by-moment to tell us exactly what to think, do, and say in every situation?

_____

_____

_____

_____

A Couple of Discernment Reminders:

• When you embark on a new path that you really sense is God's will and some people push back, be firm but gracious. Say something like: "I may not be hearing perfectly from God, but I am going this direction because at this moment, this is what I genuinely believe God is leading me to do."[1]

• Sometimes God leads us down paths that are hard or seem like big mistakes. We can't measure the will of God by how things look in the moment. If you're in that spot, follow the next thing God reveals. If you keep trusting and walking, by the end of your life (or at least in the life to come), you will be able to see how God used even those painful periods for his glory, and yours and others' good.

_____

1 If ten of your wisest, most trusted friends are discouraging your chosen course of action, that's a different story!

8. It has been said, "About ninety percent of God's will for our lives is already spelled out in his Word. The other ten percent is just details." Based on what you know of God's Word, what are some things that you know for sure are the will of God for your life today?

_____

_____

_____

_____

_____

God's Spirit

9. Read these words of Jesus:

   "When he, the Spirit of truth, comes, he will guide you into all the truth. He will not speak on his own; he will speak only what he hears, and he will tell you what is yet to come." (John 16:13)

   What is the role of the Holy Spirit in helping us discern God's truth and/or God's will?

   _____

   _____

   _____

   _____

10. In John 16, Jesus talks about "the Spirit of Truth." In John 17, Jesus says, "Your Word is truth" (v. 17). Do you think there could ever be a time when God's Spirit and God's Word would lead us in two different ways?

    _____

    _____

    _____

    _____

We want to be able to see our whole future in front of us. We'd prefer a detailed itinerary for life. Instead, God gives us a flashlight and a reliable guide. The flashlight is his Word (see Psalm 119:105), and the guide is his Spirit. That's because he wants us to "live by faith, not by sight" (2 Corinthians 5:7). We need to make our decision on what is revealed to us today. God may take us another direction tomorrow, but that's okay. Remember: God is not trying to hide his will. He wants you to know his will for you today more than you seek to know it.

Other Resources for Discerning the Will of God

Tool	Definition	Danger
Godly counsel "Plans fail for lack of counsel, but with many advisers they succeed" (Proverbs 15:22).	Seeking input and advice from spiritually wise friends and experienced mentors	▶ People are fallible and sometimes suggest wrong or unwise actions. ▶ We tend to gravitate toward those who will tell us what we want to hear.
Sovereign circumstances "We may throw the dice, but the Lord determines how they fall" (Proverbs 16:33, NLT; see also Romans 8:28 and Ecclesiastes 7:13–14).	Observing life events and prayerfully considering how God might be leading you through his providential acts	▶ Obstacles don't always mean "stop." ▶ Open doors don't always mean "go."
Holy contentment "Let the peace that comes from Christ rule in your hearts" (Colossians 3:15, NLT).	Paying close attention to your heart and to the course of action that brings an undeniable sense of "peace" and/or rightness	▶ Sometimes God's will is scary and not peaceful—consider Jesus wrestling with God's will and sweating blood in Gethsemane (Luke 22:44).
Divine compulsions "Now, compelled by the Spirit, I am going to Jerusalem, not knowing what will happen to me there" (Acts 20:22; see also Romans 8:14).	Noticing inner promptings, checks on your spirit, impressions, or "nudges" by the Holy Spirit to do (or not do) a certain thing	▶ Not every internal urge is from God. ▶ Any whim or notion needs to be prayerfully and carefully analyzed in light of God's Word—that's part of discernment!
Common sense "Good sense is a fountain of life to him who has it, but the instruction of fools is folly" (Proverbs 16:22, ESV).	Taking into account reason, facts, and logic. For example, realizing as a 6-foot 6-inch, 250-pound guy, you probably weren't meant for a career as a jockey	▶ God's ways are higher than ours. ▶ Sometimes God's ways might seem crazy. For example, having your fiancée tell you that God made her pregnant (Matthew 1:18–19)!

11. What's your experience with discerning God's will via these means?

_____

_____

_____

_____

12. How could you use these tools and resources in your current search to know God's will in a certain situation?

_____

_____

Here's a final truth about discovering the truth and/or will of God.

Truth #4: **Discerning God's will requires effort on our part.**

Much of God's will for your life is already quite clear.

> "Trust in the Lord with all your heart; do not depend on your own understanding. Seek his will in all you do, and he will show you which path to take" (Proverbs 3:5–6, NLT).

▶ You were *created* to:

✦ Glorify God (Isaiah 43:7)

✦ Love him with all your heart (Mark 12:28–30)

▶ You've been *called* to:

✦ Follow Jesus and help others learn to do likewise (Matthew 28:18–20)

▶ You're *commanded* to:

✦ Love others (John 13:34–35)

✦ Serve others with all the blessings God has given you (1 Peter 4:11).

> God always speaks clearly, but we don't always hear clearly.

Those things will always be true, no matter where you go to college, whom you marry, what career you choose, or where you decide to live. In other words, most of the "what?" is clear. All that remains now is discovering the details (How? Where? When? With whom?).

This involves cultivating the ability to use the resources God has given to develop the ability to hear God's voice and follow his specific leaning. What's your part in discovering those details?

Pray

"If any of you lacks wisdom, you should ask God, who gives generously to all without finding fault, and it will be given to you. But when you ask, you must believe and not doubt, because the one who doubts is like a wave of the sea, blown and tossed by the wind. That person should not expect to receive anything from the Lord" (James 1:5–7).

13. According to James, why is believing in God's generosity important for someone seeking God's direction?

_____

_____

_____

_____

_____

Recognize and Relinquish

Because of our unique personalities and life experiences, we each have tendencies, biases, predispositions, "default" ways of reacting, unconscious habits, and compulsive behaviors (sometimes bordering on addiction).

For example, maybe your natural instinct is to play the role of rescuer, and so you keep falling into bad relationships. Or maybe because of your own chaotic childhood you have a tendency to try to control everything about your own child's life. If so, it could be that some of your parenting decisions are rooted more in fear than in the will of God. Or maybe your high salary is less a blessing to you, and more a master—so that when the opportunity arises for you to pursue your dream job (at about half the income), you feel like you can't even consider it. You get antsy, even terrified at the thought of walking away from such a financial safety net. Maybe, in truth, it's money, not God, that's directing your life.

Whatever your particular struggle, it's important to recognize it. Only by first identifying the deep issues of your heart can you consciously relinquish those things and trust God. Some struggles are long-term, or as C. S. Lewis calls them, "afflictions." In those instances, recognizing and relinquishing is a continual process.

14. What is one tendency or natural instinct you have that probably fights against your ability to discern the will of God in your life?

_____

_____

_____

_____

Take-Home Reflections

Take Action

Someone has wisely noted that it's impossible to steer a parked car. Get moving on the clear things. Stop waiting for a detailed twenty-year plan (that's never going to drop from heaven). Instead, trust God and take a step of faith. Then another and another. All along the way, ask the Lord to guide you and re-route you if you get off course. Don't get fixated on the destination you imagine, or you will end up feeling hurt and betrayed by God.

Sometimes God leads us down paths that don't appear to turn out well. That's okay.

Just follow the next thing God reveals. By the end of your life, you will see how the painful things in life are also used by God.

Unlike the original followers of Christ, we do not have Jesus physically with us. We don't have the privilege of watching and listening to him talk in person. We live in a loud, noisy world that offers us a million options.

And so we need discernment. We need to cultivate the ability to open the Word of the Lord and be sensitive to the Spirit of the Lord. That's how we know what's true, and what we need to do.

Life Application

An important part of discipleship is learning how to apply God's truths to your life. Below are just a few ways you can start thinking about what you've learned and apply it to your daily life.

1. Memorize our verse, Romans 12:2.

2. Review the table on the next page, "When God's Will Isn't Black and White."

3. Wrestle with one or two of these questions:

   ▷ Why is it often so hard to know what is the best course of action?

   ▷ What do you think of the idea that if we are not already doing the things God has clearly shown us to do, why would he reveal any more of his will for our lives?

▷ How can other spiritual practices like solitude and silence (Topic 22) or fasting (Topic 26) be helpful in hearing God and finding guidance for life?

▷ How do you handle conflicting feelings and competing impulses?

▷ What big, confusing decisions are you facing now?

▷ If you are at a crossroads, answer these questions: What gives you a deep sense of joy, significance, and satisfaction? What habits and activities do you walk away from saying, "I sense God's pleasure every time I do that"?

▷ Do you think you have the spiritual gift of discernment?

If you love God, you'll stop in the right place even if you make mistakes along the way.

When God's Will Isn't Black and White

The Bible gives explicit instruction regarding lots of things. What about when we're facing a choice the Scriptures don't specifically address? Consider these ten principles in trying to discern what to do.

Ask Yourself	Scripture	Principle
Will this bring glory to God?	1 Corinthians 10:31	I am to live my life in such a way that God always gets the glory he deserves.
Am I trusting God, relying on my own wisdom, or trying to please someone else?	Proverbs 3:5–6, NLT; cf. 2 Corinthians 5:9–10	Biblical faith resists both the temptation to be a "men-pleaser" and the urge to rely on worldly wisdom.
Is this a case of "If it seems too good to be true, it probably is"?	Proverbs 14:12	We live in a confusing world influenced by a destructive deceiver whose goal is to ruin our lives. We should be careful and prayerful!
Could my faith be damaged or my character corrupted by this choice?	1 Corinthians 15:33	I will be influenced by environments I choose and the company I keep.
How does this square with my calling to pursue holiness?	1 Peter 1:14–15	As disciples, we are called to be different (in attitudes and actions) from those around us.
Would this decision harm Christ's reputation or my own as his disciple?	Ephesians 5:3	We must be above reproach in all we do.
Could this be the first step on the path to spiritual or moral danger?	Proverbs 4:14–15	We must be alert, recognizing the weakness of our flesh and the power of sinful desires.
Would this action send the wrong signal to a "weaker" believer who might copy my behavior and violate his or her conscience?	1 Corinthians 8:9	The law of love requires that I sometimes voluntarily (and selflessly) limit my freedom for the sake of others.
Even if this isn't "sinful," is it "wise"?	1 Corinthians 10:23	Some things are "okay," others are "good," and still others are "best." Disciples are called to pursue the best!
Do older and wiser believers agree with my chosen course of action?	Proverbs 12:17	It is foolish (and prideful) not to seek out and heed the wise counsel of godly men and women we respect when facing a tough decision.

Leader Guide

Congratulations! You've either decided to lead a discipleship group, or you're thinking hard about it. Guess what? God does big things through small groups. When his people gather together, open his Word, and invite his Spirit to work, their lives are changed!

Do you feel intimidated yet?

Be comforted by this: even the great apostle Paul felt "in over his head" at times. When he went to Corinth to help people grasp God's truth, he admitted he was overwhelmed: "I came to you in weakness with great fear and trembling" (1 Corinthians 2:3). Later he wondered, "Who is equal to such a task?" (2 Corinthians 2:16).

Feelings of inadequacy are normal; every leader has them. What's more, they're actually healthy. They keep us dependent on the Lord. It is in our times of greatest weakness that God works most powerfully. The Lord assured Paul, "My grace is sufficient for you, for my power is made perfect in weakness" (2 Corinthians 12:9).

What is the goal of a discipleship group? Listen to what Jesus said to the disciples in the verses known as the Great Commission:

"Then Jesus came to them and said, 'All authority in heaven and on earth has been given to me. Therefore go and make disciples of all nations, baptizing them in the name of the Father and of the Son and of the Holy Spirit, and teaching them to obey everything I have commanded you. And surely I am with you always, to the very end of the age'" (Matthew 28:18–20).

Discipleship is about learning to follow God and then helping others do the same. God's ultimate goal for us is that we would become like Jesus Christ. This means that this study is not about filling our heads with more information. Rather, it is about undergoing transformation. We study and apply God's truth so that it will reshape our hearts and minds, and so that over time, we will become more and more like Jesus. And the best part is, he promises to be with us throughout the whole process, giving us the strength we need as we learn to walk in his footsteps alongside our fellow believers.

How To Use This Book

This workbook is part of a three-book study of discipleship by Rose Publishing: *Rose Discipleship Series*.

▷ Knowing: Basics of the Faith

▷ Growing: Fruits of the Spirit

▷ Going: Spiritual Practices

Each book contains ten topics and can be completed in ten weeks. The books can be completed in any order—it all depends on the unique needs of your church or discipleship group.

Each session in these studies has an introduction to the session topic, followed by three sections: Bible Study, Take-Home Reflections, and Life Application. The *Introduction* familiarizes your discipleship group to the topic. The *Bible Study* section examines how that topic is related to the Christian faith. In *Take-Home Reflections*, you'll find prompts to help participants meditate on the topic during the week. Finally, the *Life Application* offers a memory verse and reading material to help group members incorporate the topic into the rhythm of everyday life.

Below are some suggestions for how to structure your discipleship group's meeting time.

	30-Minute Session	**60-Minute Session**
Introduction	Open in prayer and introduce your group to the topic for the week. Read the topic Bible verse. *5 minutes*	Open in prayer and introduce your group to the topic for the week. Discuss the topic together. *15 minutes*
Bible Study	Read this section together. Members voluntarily share their answers to the questions. *20 minutes*	Read this section together. Members voluntarily share their answers to the questions. *20 minutes*
Take-Home Reflections	Group members may go through this section on their own during the week.	Group members may go through this section on their own during the week.
Life Application	Group members may go through this section on their own during the week.	Read the memory verse. Choose one or two questions for group members to voluntarily discuss. *15 minutes*
Prayer & Closing	Conclude with a brief prayer. *5 minutes*	Ask members to share prayer requests. Conclude with prayer. *10 minutes*

Here are some important truths to keep in mind as you embark on leading a discipleship group:

▷ God is the primary agent of transformation in a person's life. You can't rescue or "fix" anyone. See yourself, instead, as a human instrument in God's hands. The Holy Spirit alone knows what is best for each person. Trust him to work his will (not yours) in his own timing.

▷ Your job description is to be pure, available, and yielded to God. You are to be a conduit of God's love, grace, and truth. Your role is to ask God to work in your group members' lives—to believe that he sees and knows the deep needs of their hearts, to trust that he is at work, even when you can't see it.

▷ Though you can't save anyone or *make* anyone grow in the faith, you can:

✦ Pray
✦ Observe
✦ Come alongside
✦ Engage
✦ Accept
✦ Invite
✦ Ask good questions
✦ Listen
✦ Model
✦ Love
✦ Serve

✦ Share the gospel
✦ Open your heart and life
✦ Pass on your experiences
✦ Invest time
✦ Teach skills
✦ Remind
✦ Encourage
✦ Challenge
✦ Gently confront
✦ Be gracious and merciful

In short, you can do a *lot!*

▷ Those who happen to be in your discipleship group are ultimately Christ's followers, not yours. They should imitate you only to the extent that you are imitating Jesus. Don't try to create clones of yourself. Everyone's personality is different. Each person approaches faith and life in ways that you might not.

▷ The spiritual success or failure of those in your group is not—ultimately—your responsibility. Your responsibility is to be faithful. *God is in charge of outcomes.* Don't take credit for "dynamic" disciples; don't shoulder excessive blame for "followers who falter or fail."

What to Expect in a Discipleship Group

Something very powerful happens when Christians who are eager to grow in their faith commit to:

- ▶ "Do life together" for a season.

- ▶ Gather regularly to open God's Word and wrestle with what it means to follow Jesus.

- ▶ Trust the Spirit of God to bring about transformation in and through them.

Here's a list of five things you can expect if you participate in a discipleship group:

1. **You'll be surprised.** When we dig deeply and ponder prayerfully, we discover things about God, about walking with Christ, and about ourselves that we never knew. Disciples should be curious and open.

2. **You'll be transformed.** Jesus promised that those who are spiritually hungry and thirsty would be satisfied (Matthew 5:6). Disciples can expect to know God better and grow in the faith.

3. **You'll be encouraged.** Nothing is more inspiring than being in a group where the members are experiencing transformation and are being used by Jesus to make an eternal difference in the world. Disciples must be committed and faithful to build each other up in the faith.

4. **You'll encounter resistance.** The enemy of our souls doesn't want us growing in the faith. He will pull out all the stops to oppose, distract, and tempt us. Disciples have to be wary and persistent.

5. **You'll be corrected.** The more we study God's Word, the more we realize that many of our notions about life and the spiritual life are simply wrong. Disciples need to be humble and teachable.

If you are up for all that, here are five important challenges:

1. **Be committed.** The old saying is true: You get out what you put in. Show up. When you miss a group meeting, others can't benefit from what God is teaching you. But don't just attend. Merely showing up to meetings doesn't lead to growing up in the faith. Study. Ponder. Wrestle. Then come prepared to participate.

2. **Be authentic.** It's always tempting to try to make ourselves look better—more spiritual, more solid, etc.—than we really are. But no one benefits from that kind of dishonesty. You don't need to share your deepest secrets, but be a truth-teller even when the truth is hard or ugly. Often one member's transparency and vulnerability can set the tone for an entire group. Be that person!

3. **Be trustworthy.** Help make the group a safe place. Adapt the "Vegas philosophy": *What's said in the group stays in the group*. Don't blab the secrets of others. There's no quicker way to kill a group.

4. **Be realistic.** Groups aren't heaven on earth. You won't "click" with everyone. Some nights the discussions will drag—or you'll come away with more questions than you had when you showed up. That's okay. Remember discipleship is a lifelong process, not an eight- or thirty-week program. Hang in there. Long journeys take a lot of little steps.

5. **Be prayerful.** Jesus said, "Apart from me, you can do nothing" (John 15:5). Without the presence of Christ, your group will be a mere meeting. But if, in a spirit of faith and surrender, you summon and submit to the infinite power of God, who knows what might happen?

Notes

Notes

Notes

Notes